Charlottesville 30

WASHINGTON

BALTIMORE

Annapolis 16

Richmond 24

Williamsburg 34

Raleigh-Durham 42

VIRGINIA
Beach 38

Charleston 48

ASHEVILLE 108

SAVANNAH
52

CAPE
Canaveral
68

St. Simons
Island 58

Palm
Beach 72

Fort
Lauderdale
76

MIAMI

Cuban
Miami
86

South
Beach 80

he Everglades
90

The New York Times

36
HOURS

The New York Times

HOURS
USA & CANADA
SOUTHEAST

TASCHEN

Contents

 # Foreword

No part of the United States has a more enduring regional culture than the South. Travelers in the sultry cities of the old Confederacy relax into a languid pace as they meander on shaded streets and sip sweet tea in white-tablecloth cafes, basking in the famed hospitality. Antiques shops and boutiques beckon passersby into fine old restored mansions. The easygoing, unrushed atmosphere seems to hold even if the office towers and business parks of the urbanized New South are just a couple of blocks away.

In the emerald valleys of the Appalachians, roads spiral toward hidden trails and waterfalls, passing crafts shops selling homemade brooms, or shoot arrow-straight to the country-branded neon of Dollywood or the Grand Ole Opry. On the coasts, sun-warmed waves, sailboat harbors, and sandy beaches make lazy afternoons almost mandatory. Even in the border state of Maryland and in politics-obsessed Washington, D.C., soft accents, grits, and gospel choirs are easy to find.

The lure of the old South feels irresistible while you're admiring the horseflesh at Churchill Downs or listening to a sweet, sad blues guitar at a bar in the Mississippi Delta. Yet while Southerners proudly preserve the best of their traditions, they are hardly clinging to the past. Their up-to-the-minute present is fascinating, too.

In the rapidly growing cities, stylish boutiques and youthful galleries are bringing stodgy or rundown old neighborhoods back to vibrant life. Spas and yoga studios operate in the shadow of the Blue Ridge. Night life was never hipper than it is in Miami's South Beach. Museums of slavery and civil rights look the dark side of the past straight in the eye. And innovative chefs reinterpret the rich regional cuisine

into dishes like organic lamb with braised collard greens or crawfish and andouille cheesecake. In some cities' restaurant rows, foie gras is as common as fried chicken.

The 33 itineraries in this book span the wealth of America's Southeast, laying out a selection of weekend adventures from Annapolis to New Orleans. All are adapted — always with updating, and often with new material specifically for the book — from the 36 Hours column in The New York Times, a travel feature that has been inspiring trips, wish lists, and clip-and-saves for a decade. Created as a guide to that staple of crammed 21st-century schedules, the weekend getaway, 36 Hours takes readers each week on a carefully researched, uniquely designed two-night excursion to an embraceable place. It guides readers to an experience that both identifies the high points of the destination and teases out its particular character. From the beginning, 36 Hours has been a hit with readers.

In late 2011, The New York Times and TASCHEN published The New York Times 36 Hours: 150 Weekends in the U.S.A. & Canada, which gathered together 150 North American 36 Hours columns in one volume. In 2012, the decision was made to offer this trove of travel guidance in another format: as five regional books, each easily portable and specifically focused, to meet the needs of a traveler who wants to concentrate on one area at a time. This book is one of the five; the others are devoted to the Northeast, the Midwest and Great Lakes, the Southwest and Rocky Mountains, and the West Coast including Alaska and Hawaii.

The work of hundreds of writers, photographers, graphic artists, designers, and editors, combining their creativity over many years, has gone into 36 Hours and into this book. Their individual talents are reflected in the styles and selections they have chosen. But essentially, a 36 Hours is not about a writer's travels at all, but about a trip the traveler can take. The Southeast offers a plenitude of interesting roaming. So why not get started? All you need is a weekend.

— BARBARA IRELAND, EDITOR

PAGE 2 The surf, sand, and towers of Miami Beach, Florida, a favorite setting for the great American vacation.

PAGE 4 The Lincoln Memorial in Washington: a shrine to freedom in a city of monuments.

OPPOSITE A thoroughbred at home amid the black rail fences of the Kentucky Bluegrass Country around Lexington.

Tips for Using This Book

Plotting the Course: Travelers don't make their way through a region or a country alphabetically, and this book doesn't proceed that way, either. It begins in a major city emblematic of the region and winds from place to place the way a touring adventurer on a car trip might. An alphabetical index appears at the end of the book.

On the Ground: Every *36 Hours* follows a workable numbered itinerary, which is both outlined in the text and shown with corresponding numbers on a detailed destination map. The itinerary is practical: it really is possible to get from one place to the next easily and in the allotted time, although of course many travelers will prefer to take things at their own pace and perhaps take some of their own detours. Astute readers will notice that the "36" in *36 Hours* is elastic, and the traveler's agenda probably will be, too.

The Not So Obvious: The itineraries do not all follow exactly the same pattern. A restaurant for Saturday breakfast may or may not be recommended; after-dinner night life may be included or may not. The destination dictates, and so, to some extent, does the personality of the author who researched and wrote the article. In large cities, where it is impossible to see everything in a weekend, the emphasis is on the less expected discovery over the big, highly promoted attraction that is already well known.

Seasons: The time of year to visit is left up to the traveler, but in general, the big cities are good anytime; towns where snow falls are usually best visited in warm months, unless they are ski destinations; and summer heat is more or less endurable depending on the traveler's own tolerance. The most tourist-oriented areas are often seasonal—some of the sites featured in vacation towns may be closed out of season.

Your Own Agenda: This book is not a conventional guidebook. A *36 Hours* is meant to give a well-informed inside view of each place it covers, a selective summary that lets the traveler get to the heart of things in minimal time. Travelers who have more days to spend may want to use a *36 Hours* as a kind of nugget, supplementing it with the more comprehensive information available on bookstore shelves or on the locally sponsored Internet sites where towns and regions offer exhaustive lists of their attractions. Or, two or three of these itineraries can easily be strung together to make up a longer trip.

Updates: While all the stories in this volume were updated and fact-checked for publication in fall 2011, it is inevitable that some of the featured businesses and destinations will change in time. If you spot any errors in your travels, please feel free to send corrections or updates via email to 36hoursamerica@taschen.com. Please include "36 Hours Correction" and the page number in the subject line of your email to assure that it gets to the right person for future updates.

OPPOSITE The French Quarter, New Orleans.

THE BASICS

A brief informational box for the destination, called "The Basics," appears with each *36 Hours* article in this book. The box provides some orientation on transportation for that location, including whether a traveler arriving by plane should rent a car to follow the itinerary. "The Basics" also recommends three reliable hotels or other lodgings.

PRICES

Since hotel and restaurant prices change quickly, this book uses a system of symbols, based on 2011 United States dollars.

Hotel room, standard double:
Budget, under $100 per night: $
Moderate, $100 to $199: $$
Expensive, $200 to $299: $$$
Luxury, $300 and above: $$$$

Restaurants, dinner without wine:
Budget, under $15: $
Moderate, $16 to $24: $$
Expensive, $25 to $49: $$$
Very Expensive, $50 and up: $$$$

Restaurants, full breakfast, or lunch entree:
Budget, under $8: $
Moderate, $8 to $14: $$
Expensive, $15 to $24: $$$
Very Expensive, $25 and up: $$$$

Washington D.C.

The familiar monuments, symbols, and sites of Washington are American icons no visitor should miss. But there are times on a Washington weekend when it's best to leave the imperial city and spend some time with the people who live here full time. They're not all politicians, but a Washingtonian without some political connection can be hard to find. So stay alert. Someone may be trading insider gossip at the next restaurant table. — BY HELENE COOPER

FRIDAY

1 *House Party* 6 p.m.

Hobnob with the Beltway crowd at **Eighteenth Street Lounge** (1212 18th Street NW; 202-466-3922; eighteenthstreetlounge.com). Enter through the door next to the Mattress Discounters—there's no sign outside—take the stairs, and voila! A multilevel row house, with room after room of velvet couches and fireplaces, awaits you. There's a back deck for spring and summer after-work cocktails, and the crowd is a mix of political activists and Middle Eastern and European World Bank types.

2 *Eat like Oprah* 8 p.m.

Take a taxi to **Capitol Hill**, to **Art and Soul Restaurant** in the Liaison Hotel (415 New Jersey Avenue NW; 202-393-7777; artandsouldc.com; $$$). Oprah Winfrey's former chef, Art Smith, owns this restaurant, and it does a big business in D.C. parties. Yes, you've already had a cocktail, but you're not driving, so be sure to try the margarita at the bar before sitting down to eat. The menu will remind you that Washington is a Southern city. Sprinkled among the more usual listings, like seared ahi tuna and arugula salad, you'll see preparations like "country fried" and "red-eye" and foods like ribs, okra, watermelon pickles, and collard greens. Not to mention the fried green tomatoes.

3 *Freedom Walk* 10 p.m.

With luck, no one in your party wore the five-inch Prada heels tonight, because you're about to walk off that pork chop as you head down the National Mall. Your destination is the **Lincoln Memorial** (nps.gov/linc), with ole Abe backlit at night. Washington's monument row is always best viewed at night,

when the tourists are gone and the romantics are strolling arm in arm. The Lincoln Memorial, long the first destination for African-American visitors to Washington, has often been an emotionally charged spot: think of Marian Anderson's concert in 1939, Martin Luther King's "I Have a Dream" speech, and Election Night 2008, when Illinois learned it was sending another of its sons to Washington. In quieter times it is almost a retreat, as residents and visitors alike come to read the inscription "With malice toward none, with charity for all" and to ponder America the Beautiful.

SATURDAY

4 *Morning Sit-in* 9 a.m.

Breakfast at **Florida Avenue Grill** (1100 Florida Avenue NW; 202-265-1586; floridaavenuegrill.com; $), a soul food institution, is a dip into the past, evoking the feel of lunch counter sit-ins and the civil rights movement. The place has been serving greasy and delicious Southern cooking since 1944. Buttery grits,

OPPOSITE Inside the Capitol Hill Visitor Center, where guests can see the Capitol Dome peering through a large glass ceiling.

BELOW The Lincoln Memorial at night.

Virginia ham, biscuits and gravy, even scrapple — all surrounded by photos of past Washington bigwigs as various as Ron Brown, the former commerce secretary, and Strom Thurmond, the former South Carolina senator.

5 *1600 Pennsylvania* 10 a.m.

We know. It's the ultimate in touristy. But come on, it's the **White House** (1600 Pennsylvania Avenue; 202-456-7041; whitehouse.gov). To schedule a public tour, first you'll need to find nine friends to come with you. Then call your Congressional representative to schedule. (Not sure who? Go to writerep.house.gov.) These self-guided tours — which are allotted on a first-come-first-served basis about one month before

the requested date — allow you to explore the public rooms and the gardens. Sorry, you won't be able to check out the decorating in the first family's private quarters, but you will get to see the East Room, the Diplomatic Reception Room, and the dining room where they have those swanky state dinners.

6 *Hello, Betsy* Noon

No, not that Betsy…there are no star-spangled banners at **Betsy Fisher** (1224 Connecticut Avenue NW; 202-785-1975; betsyfisher.com). This stylish and

ABOVE Ben's Chili Bowl on U Street Northwest, popular by day and an institution late at night.

BELOW The chorus at St. Augustine Roman Catholic Church at 15th and V Streets Northwest, one of the oldest black Catholic churches in the country.

OPPOSITE A view of the Capitol from down the Mall.

funky boutique is port of call for those well-dressed deputies in the White House. The owner, Betsy Fisher Albaugh, always has cocktails and wine on hand to occupy the men who invariably are dragged into the store.

7 *Go Represent* 2 p.m.

It took six years to complete, but the **U.S. Capitol Visitor Center** (Capitol Hill; at the east end of the Mall; 202-225-6827; visitthecapitol.gov) finally opened at the end of 2007. The subterranean center is meant to relieve the bottleneck that used to serve as the entryway for visitors to the Capitol. It does that and more, although some critics say it assumes a life of its own that is too separate from the Capitol itself. See for yourself — you can book a tour via the Web site, or just show up and wander around. The center has a rotating display of historic documents that can range from a ceremonial copy of the 13th Amendment, abolishing slavery, to the speech President George W. Bush delivered to Congress after the Sept. 11 attacks.

8 *Political Dish* 7 p.m.

O.K., enough with the federal touring, it's time to hang out with the real Washingtonians. Head to the always hopping **U Street Corridor**, and plop yourself on a stool at **Local 16** (1602 U Street NW; 202-265-2828; localsixteen.com). There are multiple lounges and, best of all, a roof deck where you can see the city

lights while you sip your pre-dinner watermelon martini. Have dinner a few blocks away at **Cork Wine Bar** (1720 14th Street NW; 202-265-2675; corkdc.com; $$), which might have the best fries in town. The menu includes both small and big bites, from marinated olives and cheeses to duck confit and sautéed kale. And for goodness' sake, don't forget those fries! They are tossed with garlic and lemon. In fact, order two helpings.

9 *Smoke-filled Room* 10:30 p.m.

Puff away the rest of your evening at **Chi-Cha** (1624 U Street NW; 202-234-8400; latinconcepts.com/chicha.php), a hookah lounge where you can smoke honey tobacco out of a water pipe and sip late-night cocktails. The eclectic crowd dances to rumba and slow salsa into the wee hours, and there's always a diplomat in a corner couch doing something inappropriate — avert your eyes, enjoy your hookah, and sway to the beat. You could be in Beirut. O.K., let's try that one again. You could be in Marrakesh. Well, maybe Marrakesh with Brazilian music. If you want to keep the night going, stop by **Ben's Chili Bowl** (1213 U Street NW; 202-667-0909; benschilibowl.com), a Washington institution so established that even President Nicolas Sarkozy of France has stopped by for the Chili Half-Smoke hot dogs. He went at noon, but Ben's is busiest in the wee hours.

SUNDAY

10 *River Idyll* 8 a.m.

Washington is known for beautiful mornings along the Potomac River, especially on the water. **Thompson Boat Center** (2900 Virginia Avenue NW; 202-333-9543; thompsonboatcenter.com), just where Georgetown meets Rock Creek Parkway, offers canoe rentals. Paddle up the river, and you might catch a senator (or a Saudi prince) having coffee on the patio of a stately home.

11 *Lift Your Voice* 12:30 p.m.

St. Augustine Roman Catholic Church (1419 V Street NW; 202-265-1470; saintaugustine-dc.org), which calls itself "the Mother Church of Black Catholics in the United States" is one of the oldest black Catholic churches in the country. The 12:30 Sunday Mass combines traditional black spirituals with gospel music. The place rocked with particular fervor after Inauguration Day 2009.

ABOVE Outside the White House, which is off-limits to walk-ins. Group tours are allowed, but they must be arranged a month in advance.

OPPOSITE The Capitol as seen through a window at the Library of Congress.

THE BASICS

Washington's two airports are well served by an array of airlines. The subway, usually called the Metro, has multiple convenient stops.

Hotel Monaco
700 F Street NW
202-628-7177
monaco-dc.com
$$$-$$$$
A Kimpton hotel in the Penn Quarter neighborhood across from the National Portrait Gallery and near the International Spy Museum.

Hotel Palomar
2121 P Street NW
202-448-1800
hotelpalomar-dc.com
$$$-$$$$
Another Kimpton boutique hotel, in the heart of Dupont Circle.

Hotel Tabard Inn
1739 N Street NW
202-785-1277
tabardinn.com
$$
A budget alternative filled with charm. Some rooms share baths.

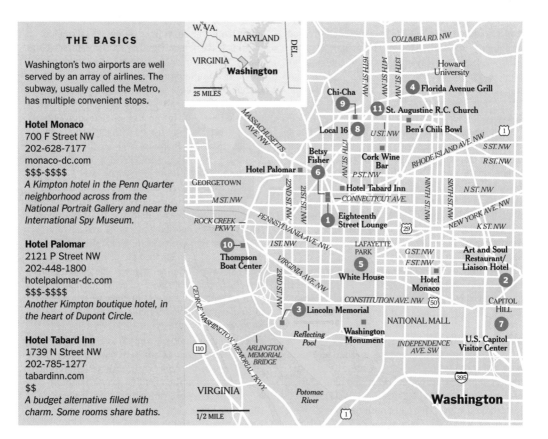

Annapolis

Spring comes to Annapolis, Maryland, on a perfumed cloud of burning wool. Every year at the vernal equinox, boaters in this sailing-mad community on the Chesapeake Bay gather on City Dock to create a bonfire of their winter socks, signaling a bare-toed welcome to the official start of the sailing season. What remains after the smoke clears is a stunningly beautiful village well worth a weekend excursion. Annapolis has undeniable historic importance—it was here that George Washington resigned his commission as commander in chief in 1783, and the city briefly served as the nation's capital. It has been the home of the United States Naval Academy since the academy's founding in 1845. But its charms are not simply academic. It is an architecturally rich, compact town (population about 36,000) made for strolling, where a walk along the waterfront on a sunny afternoon can wipe away the stress of the past work week and where a turn down a small side street can take you back two centuries in time.
— BY STUART EMMRICH

FRIDAY

1 *Sunset on the Dock* 7 p.m.

Start your weekend the way the locals do: with a sunset walk along **City Dock**, in the heart of downtown. Have a quick chat with one of the dozens of sailors getting their small boats ready for a trip out on the water on Saturday. Yachtsmen proudly parade their boats on the finger of water that ends at the dock—so proudly that it has gained the name Ego Alley. Pop into **Storm Bros. Ice Cream Factory** (130 Dock Street; stormbros.com) for a cone or a chocolate malt. Or go across to **Pusser's Carribean Grille** (80 Compromise Street; 410-626-0004; pussersusa.com/locations/annapolis-restaurant) for a beer on its outdoor deck. Like many things in Annapolis, its name has a story. Pusser's was the brand of rum that kept British sailors going on the high seas for hundreds of years.

OPPOSITE The rotunda of Bancroft Hall, the 1.4 million-square-foot dormitory at the United States Naval Academy. All 4,400 midshipmen live in this mammoth building.

RIGHT The exterior of the Academy's chapel. Inside is the crypt of John Paul Jones.

2 *Fusion Infusion* 8 p.m.

The venerable **Middleton Tavern** (2 Market Space; first opened in 1750) is a dinner standby on the dock, often crowded with tourists. For a different experience, walk a few blocks to **Aqua Terra** (164 Main Street; 410-263-1985; aquaterraofannapolis.com; $$-$$$), where fusion cuisine has elbowed its way into the land of clam chowder and crab cakes. The menu changes seasonally, but the emphasis is on sushi, small plates (think potstickers, sliders, and jambalaya) and imaginatively prepared sides for the meats and fish. A well-received newer spot, back at the dock, is **Hell Point Seafood** (12 Dock Street; 410-990-9888; hp-seafood.com; $$-$$$), opened in 2009 by Bob Kinkead, a renowned Washington chef.

3 *Walk Back in Time* 10 p.m.

Take a late evening stroll down **Prince George Street**. Though you will probably want to come back for a daytime view of these spectacular examples of mid-19th-century architecture (Greek Revival town houses, Italianate mansions), there is something particularly evocative about seeing these homes at night, when the streets are empty of cars and tourist-laden horse-drawn carriages, and the vibrantly colored living rooms (deep greens and rich, dark reds) are illuminated by antique lamps.

SATURDAY

4 *Greeting the Day* 8:30 a.m.

Return to the dock, where last night's crowd has been replaced by young families and dog owners

taking their pets out for an early morning walk, and have an al fresco breakfast of a pastry and coffee from **Hard Bean Coffee & Book Sellers** (36 Market Space; 410-263-8770).

5 *18th-Century Splendor* 10 a.m.

One of the most impressive homes in Annapolis is the **William Paca House** (186 Prince George Street; 410-267-7619; annapolis.org), a five-part brick mansion built in 1765 and painstakingly restored two centuries later. Take a walk through the house and then wander through the formal gardens. Afterward, head up to Maryland Avenue, and keep going until you get to the **Maryland State House**. Though the State House can lay claim to being the oldest state legislative building still in use, the tour of the chambers inside can be skipped. Instead, circle around the grounds and take in a sweeping view of the Annapolis skyline from the vantage point of the building's rear balcony.

6 *Picnic on a Campus* 1 p.m.

Stop in at **Re-Sails** (42 Randall Street; 410-263-4982; resails.com) to look over the bags and backpacks made from recycled sails. Then pick up a freshly made gourmet sandwich (prosciutto and provolone, or maybe turkey with brie and apples)

BELOW A carriage navigates the winding streets of downtown Annapolis.

OPPOSITE The showy parade of yachts at the end of downtown's City Dock has earned it the name Ego Alley.

at the **Big Cheese** (47 Randall Street; 410-263-6915; $) and walk up Prince George Street to **St. John's College**, where you can have an impromptu picnic on the campus lawn, with its eye-catching views of the Severn River. St. John's, Annapolis's "other college" (and the older one, dating back to 1696) is a sort of academic antithesis of the Naval Academy. It has no majors, no departments, no written exams, and few lectures; instead, teachers guide students as they read and discuss 130 "great books" by authors as diverse as Plato and Jane Austen. The two schools face off annually in a croquet game that draws as many as 2,000 spectators. St. John's usually wins.

7 *The High Seas* 3 p.m.

Experience the bracing winds off the Chesapeake Bay from the top deck of a sightseeing boat. Forty-minute boat tours of **Annapolis Harbor** (410-268-7601; watermarkcruises.com) leave from the far end of City Dock several times a day in the warm-weather months. Longer cruises, including an all-day journey that takes you to the quaint village of St. Michaels, Maryland, are also available on weekends. A jauntier option is a two-hour schooner cruise (Woodwind Cruises; 410-263-7837; schoonerwoodwind.com).

8 *Dinner and a View* 6:30 p.m.

As the sun begins to set, walk across the **Compromise Street Bridge** to the residential neighborhood of Eastport. Turn left on Severn and then left again on First Street, and walk down to the waterfront. Here, on a small wooden bench overlooking a 10-foot-long strip of sand, you can take in some of the best views of the Naval Academy and of the sailboats coming into harbor after a day out on the sea. Then double back to Severn, and turn right and then left on Third Street for dinner at **O'Learys Seafood Restaurant** (310 Third Street; 410-263-0884; olearysseafood.com; $$$). This elegant establishment is a world away (and twice as expensive) as the chowder houses back at the Annapolis dock. But the snapper, swordfish, mahi-mahi, and their many relatives make it worth the tab.

9 *Variety Show* 8 p.m.

Rams Head On Stage (33 West Street; 410-268-4545; ramsheadtavern.com/annapolis/

onstage.html), a concert venue in the Rams Head Tavern, books nationally known musicians representing genres from acid jazz to pop, rock, R&B, country, and soul. The list of past performers runs from Ladysmith Black Mambazo to Doc Hochman's Mardi Gras Dixieband, with many stops in between. (Check the schedule and consider ordering tickets in advance.)

SUNDAY

10 *Dress Blues* 9:30 a.m.

Early Sunday morning is among the best times to take a tour of the **United States Naval Academy**. The crowds have not yet begun to stream onto the 383-acre campus, and while the chapel (which contains the crypt of John Paul Jones) will not officially be open to visitors until 1 p.m., there is something undeniably stirring about seeing the midshipmen in their dress blues streaming out of church after the Sunday service. Enter the grounds at Gate 1 at Randall and King George Streets; the excellent Armel-Leftwich Visitor Center is just inside. Particularly worth seeing as you tour the grounds: the outsize Bancroft Hall, where all 4,400 midshipmen live; the row of elegant captains' houses on Porter Street; and the riverside walk along Dewey Field.

THE BASICS

Fly into Baltimore-Washington International Airport, drive from Washington, or arrive at City Dock in your boat. Downtown Annapolis is better for walking than for driving.

Historic Inns of Annapolis
58 State Circle
410-263-2641
historicinnsofannapolis.com
$$
Three sister hotels in restored historic buildings. Period touches like wing chairs or four-poster beds.

Marriott Annapolis Waterfront
80 Compromise Street
888-773-0786
annapolismarriott.com
$$$-$$$$
City or Chesapeake Bay waterfront views.

Loews Annapolis Hotel
126 West Street
410-263-7777
loewshotels.com/en/Annapolis-Hotel
$$
Colorful and modern decor, lounge, and spa.

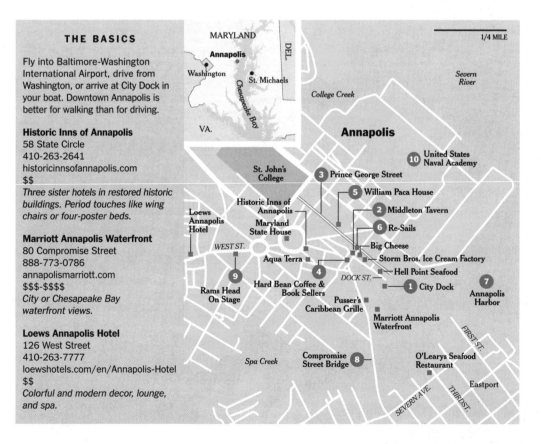

Baltimore

Baltimore's Inner Harbor, reclaimed from a nadir of rotting piers and warehouses in the 1970s, shines with office towers and hotels, an aquarium and science center, historic ships, and the nearby Camden Yards ballpark. Water taxis connect the Inner Harbor to the row houses, shops, and sometimes rowdy bars of Fell's Point, where the city began. Away from the tourist hubs, urban renewal continues in a more spontaneous form, led by artists in search of cheap rents and warehouse spaces. Once rough neighborhoods have been taken over by studios, galleries, and performance spaces. Crab joints and sports bars share cobblestone streets with fancy cafes and tapas restaurants. And with a little exploration, it's still easy to find the beehive hairdos and wacky museums that fit an old Baltimore nickname, "Charm City." — BY JOSHUA KURLANTZICK

FRIDAY

1 *Into the Woods* 3 p.m.

Though you wouldn't guess it if your only view of Baltimore were from Interstate 95, which passes port terminals and factories spewing smoke, the center of the city conceals a wooded, stream-filled oasis, the **Jones Falls Trail** (baltimorecity.gov). Designed for hiking and biking, it parallels the Jones Falls River and meanders past some of the old mills that once powered Baltimore's economy. It is a rustic and historical look at a sometimes gritty city. Enter at the northern border of Druid Hill Park and head north. Bicycle rentals are at **Light Street Cycles** (1124 Light Street; 410-685-2234; lightstcycles.com).

2 *Crabs and More* 7 p.m.

In a town known for crab cakes and fried fish sandwiches, **Woodberry Kitchen** (2010 Clipper Park Road; 410-464-8000; woodberrykitchen.com; $$$) stands out for its refined local cooking. Set in the Clipper Mill complex, an old foundry that is now an artists' haven, Woodberry serves American comfort food using seasonal and local ingredients,

OPPOSITE The old port city of Baltimore has waterfront enough for Sunday sailors, oceangoing cargo ships, and tourist hordes.

RIGHT The Inner Harbor, where recreation reigns.

like Chesapeake soft-shell crabs served with a spicy tartar sauce or cider-glazed roasted chicken atop a Spanish-style tortilla.

3 *Very Off Broadway* 10 p.m.

For offbeat theater, take a seat at the **Creative Alliance at the Patterson** (3134 Eastern Avenue; 410-276-1651; creativealliance.org), whose stage feels like an old vaudeville house. One night, you might catch burlesque artists stripping down to their pasties; another night, a documentary on Baltimore's decaying schools. The adjacent gallery often features the works of local painters and photographers.

SATURDAY

4 *Underground Cafe* 9 a.m.

Tucked into a basement of an apartment house in the row house neighborhood of Charles Village, near the main campus of Johns Hopkins University, **Carma's Café** (32nd and Saint Paul Streets; 410-243-5200; carmascafe.com; $$) is easy to miss. But neighbors flock to it for buttery cherry-almond scones, fried cheesecake (could a dessert be richer?), frittatas and salads, and innovative coffee drinks like the zamboni, a drinkable version of a snowball.

5 *Sister Act* 11 a.m.

A short walk from Carma's, the **Baltimore Museum of Art** (10 Art Museum Drive; 443-573-1700; artbma.org) has a surprisingly large endowment of post-Impressionist art. The Cone sisters, socialites who lived in Baltimore in the early 20th century, had the foresight to buy thousands of paintings by

the likes of Cézanne, Picasso, and Matisse. They willed the pieces to the museum, for whenever "the status of appreciation of modern art in Baltimore should improve." Apparently it did. Today, the Cone Collection, including Matisse's *Blue Nude* and Gauguin's *Woman of the Mango*, is the heart of the museum. When you're done inside, grab a snack at Gertrude's, the museum's restaurant, and sit at a table in the nearby sculpture garden.

6 *Call It Fell's* 1 p.m.

Explore the patisseries, bars, and galleries of Fell's Point, still a real neighborhood of Baltimore's iconic brick row houses. Start at the open-air plaza at the bottom of Broadway, where skateboarders mix with musicians and couples snuggle on benches. Walk east, along Thames Street, looking over the water. Stop to inhale French pastry at **Bonaparte Breads** (903 South Ann Street; 410-342-4000) before heading on toward Canton, the next waterfront neighborhood, full of restored warehouses turned into shops and condos.

7 *T-shirts Meet Beehives* 4 p.m.

In recent years, the neighborhood of Hampden has gone from working-class to artsy. Packed with galleries and used-clothing stores, Hampden's main drag, a part of 36th Street, called "The Avenue," is where you'll see 20-somethings in stylishly rumpled

vintage jeans sharing cigarettes with "Hons," the nickname for women who wear classic beehive hairdos. (They're celebrated every June in Baltimore's "Honfest.") For obscure self-published art books and zines, browse through **Atomic Books** (3620 Falls Road; 410-662-4444; atomicbooks.com). Then head to **In Watermelon Sugar** (3555 Chestnut Avenue; 410-662-9090), where you'll find decidedly un-Ikea furniture. You might finish up at **Minás** (815 West 36th Street; 410-732-4258; minasgalleryandboutique.com) for vintage wear, poetry readings, and the work of Baltimore-based artists.

8 *Welcome to Dinner* 7:30 p.m.

Every city needs a neighborhood restaurant that feels like a social club. In Baltimore, that would be **Petit Louis** (4800 Roland Avenue; 410-366-9393; petitlouis.com; $$$), a cozy French bistro in the affluent residential neighborhood of Roland Park. It has the air of a private party, with a host greeting diners by name and the kitchen serving up classic bistro dishes like grilled salmon with asparagus. Don't miss the pommes frites, crispy and sinfully fatty.

9 *Brew Crew* 10 p.m.

There may be tons of bars in Baltimore, but calling the **Brewer's Art** (1106 North Charles Street; 410-547-6925; thebrewersart.com) a bar is like calling crabs just another shellfish. Housed in a classic town house, the pub takes its beers very seriously, pouring everything from Trappist ales from Belgium to local microbrews like Clipper City Pale Ale. The crowd seems just as serious — artists and designers, older couples coming from the symphony, and occasional college students looking out of place among the adults.

SUNDAY

10 *The Age of Sail* 10 a.m.

Get a glimpse of authentic maritime history before midday crowds take over at the Inner Harbor. The well-maintained sloop-of-war *Constellation* (410-539-1797; constellation.org), the last all-sail ship built by the Navy and a veteran of the Civil War, is the star of several museum ships at anchor. Before the war, the *Constellation* patrolled the waters off West

Africa to block slave traders. Explore the sleeping quarters, galley, and cannons. Sailing ships once ruled this harbor. Now the craft you see may include paddle boats in the shape of Chessie, the local version of the Loch Ness monster.

11 *Young Artists* Noon

Everyone's got to start somewhere, and for many of Baltimore's top artists, that push came from the **Maryland Institute College of Art** (1300 West Mount Royal Avenue; 410-669 9200; mica.edu). The college, situated in the stately Bolton Hill neighborhood, regularly showcases the work of its promising students and faculty, which is to say the art can be hit or miss. But, as in any treasure hunt, that's part of the fun. If you're hungry, grab a bite at **b** (1501 Bolton Street; 410-383-8600; b-bistro.com; $$), a

simple bistro opened by a brother of Hamid Karzai, the president of Afghanistan. Who says Baltimore's reputation as an inviting spot hasn't gotten around?

OPPOSITE ABOVE A Dalton Ghetti pencil-tip sculpture at the American Visionary Art Museum.

OPPOSITE BELOW The cheese plate at Petit Louis.

ABOVE Cafe Hon anchors "The Avenue" in Hampden, whose pink flamingoes, beehived ladies, and classic cars were made famous through the films of John Waters.

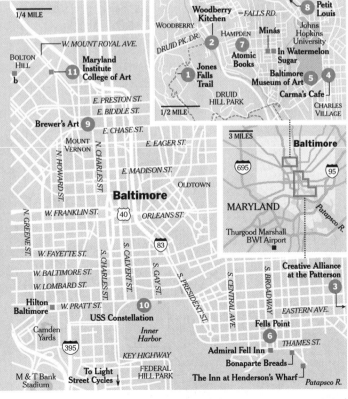

THE BASICS

By car, Baltimore is three and a half hours from New York and less than an hour from Washington, D.C. Amtrak trains are faster. Flights land at Thurgood Marshall BWI Airport. Water taxis serve harborside stops.

Admiral Fell Inn
888 South Broadway
866-583-4162
harbormagic.com
$$$
Eighty rooms in red-brick buildings from the late 18th century.

Hilton Baltimore
401 West Pratt Street
443-573-8700
baltimore.hilton.com
$$$
Downtown, with 757 rooms.

The Inn at Henderson's Wharf
1000 Fell Street
800-522-2088
hendersonswharf.com
$$$
Charm and comfort in an old tobacco factory.

Richmond

As the heart of the old Confederacy, Richmond, Virginia, will always have a claim as the capital of the South, a place to find Southern tradition and a center of Civil War history. But for decades in the late 20th century, it watched with envy as cities like Atlanta and Charlotte leaped ahead economically and culturally. Now Richmond is surging back to life in the present. A building boom in the last few years has seen century-old tobacco warehouses transformed into lofts and art studios. Chefs are setting up kitchens in formerly gritty neighborhoods. And the city's once buttoned-up downtown has life after dusk, thanks to new bars and a performing arts complex, Richmond CenterStage. Without forfeiting all of its Old South personality, Richmond now is a player in the New South, too.

— BY JUSTIN BERGMAN AND LINDSAY MORAN

FRIDAY

1 *Tea and Wisteria* 2 p.m.

For a sense of what makes Richmond Richmond, take a drive in the Fan District, so named because its wisteria- and tree-lined streets spread out like a fan. Park the car and walk along Monument Avenue, one of the loveliest places anywhere for an urban stroll. The monuments are statues — of Robert E. Lee, Stonewall Jackson, J.E.B. Stuart, and Jefferson Davis — sharing space somewhat incongruously with a more recent favorite son, Arthur Ashe Jr., the tennis champion. The stately houses are Queen Anne, Victorian, Tudor, Colonial, Italianate, Greek Revival. To complete the genteel experience, take afternoon tea, with scones and finger sandwiches, in the **Jefferson Hotel** (101 West Franklin Street; 804-788-8000; jeffersonhotel.com), whose grand style dates back to 1895.

2 *Fast Forward* 5 p.m.

Jump into the 21st century in Carytown, where shoppers and people watchers make their way to a half-mile stretch of boutiques, vintage clothing stores, and cafes. This colorful strip is Richmond at its most eclectic, mixing floppy-haired musicians, gay hipsters with pierced eyebrows, and suburban mothers pushing strollers. Check out local T-shirt designs at the **Need Supply Company** (3010 West Cary Street;

804-355-5880; needsupply.com). Examine the retro ball gowns, tiaras, and cigarette cases at **Bygones** (2916 West Cary Street; 804-353-1919; bygonesvintage.com). Or seek Japanese anime, underground graphic novels, and comics at **Chop Suey Books** (2913 West Cary Street; 804-422-8066; chopsueybooks.com).

3 *Fed in Virginia* 8 p.m.

The locavore movement was late in coming to Richmond, but residents have taken to it in a big way at the perpetually packed **Mezzanine** (3433 West Cary Street; 804-353-2186; mezzanine3433.com; $$). Produce, meats, and seafood come from Virginia farmers and fishermen. Check the ever-changing, seven-foot-tall chalkboard menu, and expect dishes like green curry quinoa with gingered bok choy and oyster mushrooms. A downside: the outdoor patio looks out over a pair of glowing golden arches across the street.

4 *Cash Bar* 10 p.m.

Richmonders used to flee downtown for the suburbs come 6 p.m. Now young politicos migrate from the nearby State Capitol to gather at **Bank** (1005 East Main Street; 804-648-3070; bankandvault.com), a century-old bank that's been transformed into a swank night spot, complete with a bar made with the building's original marble, a martini lounge in the old

OPPOSITE The Fan District, a bastion of old Richmond.

BELOW Belle Isle, now an island park accessible by footbridge from the bank of the James River, was used as a prison camp during the Civil War.

president's office, and a cavernous downstairs club, Vault. Eavesdrop at the bar and you might pick up some juicy political gossip.

SATURDAY

5 *Three-Sided War* 10 a.m.

A few diehards still call the Civil War the War of Northern Aggression, but the **American Civil War Center at Historic Tredegar** (500 Tredegar Street; 804-780-1865; tredegar.org) takes a less pro-Southern

ABOVE The American Civil War Center, which tells the story of the war from the three different perspectives of the Union, the South, and the slave population, is in the old Tredegar Gun Foundry.

approach. With interactive displays, it tells the story of the war from three perspectives: those of the Union, the Confederacy, and the slaves. The museum building itself is a giant relic, the old 1861 Tredegar Gun Foundry, a major munitions factory during the war. At the adjacent **Richmond National Battlefield Park** (nps.gov/rich), recorded voices read written wartime accounts by local witnesses, including Garland H. White, a former slave who tells of entering defeated Richmond as a Union soldier and being reunited with his mother, "an aged woman," from whom he had been sold as a small boy.

6 *Battle of the Lunch* Noon

There's a new war being waged at the **Black Sheep** (901 West Marshall Street; 804-648-1300; theblacksheeprva.com; $$), a cozy restaurant with barn-wood wainscoting and church pews for benches. Brave eaters attack two-foot-long subs named after Civil War-era ships in what the menu calls the "War of Northern Ingestion." Served on French baguettes,

the CSS Virginia is topped with fried chicken livers, shredded cabbage, and apples, while the USS Brooklyn has jerk barbecued chicken and banana ketchup. A warning: each behemoth can feed at least two.

7 *Into the Trees* 2 p.m.

Need an adrenaline boost? How about maneuvering through the trees like Tarzan? Across the James River in the Stratford Hills section, instructors at **Riverside Outfitters** (6836 Old Westham Road; 804-560-0068; riversideoutfitters.net) lead expeditions that include zip lines and harnessed walks along limbs 40 feet above the ground. Expect to pay at least $150 for two hours. If you prefer lower altitudes — and prices — stay on the Capitol side of the river and find **Belle Isle** (jamesriverpark.org), an island accessible by footbridge from Tredegar Street. It's crisscrossed with trails and offers views of Richmond's natural urban rapids, where you are likely to see intrepid kayakers. Used as a prison camp in the Civil War, the island once held 8,000 captured Union soldiers.

8 *Haute Home Cookin'* 7 p.m.

The industrial-chic bistro **LuLu's** (21 North 17th Street; 804-343-9771; lu-lusrichmond.com; $$) provides comfort food done right to the polo-shirt-wearing young professionals who have moved into the historic neighborhood of Shockoe Bottom, occupying lofts in renovated tobacco warehouses.

Scan the LuLu's menu for easygoing dishes like chicken and dumplings or a pork chop with grilled macaroni and cheese.

9 *Uptown Music* 9 p.m.

You can stay in Shockoe Bottom for drinks and dancing as its nightclubs begin to fill up. But for a quieter evening, head uptown to the **Camel** (1621 West Broad Street; 804-353-4901; thecamel.org), a venue to catch up-and-coming Southern rock and bluegrass bands, acoustic singer-songwriters, and jazz and funk musicians.

SUNDAY

10 *Havana Breakfast* 10 a.m.

Don't expect to find amazing ethnic food in Richmond — this is fried okra country, not an immigrant town. The one exception is **Kuba Kuba** (1601 Park Avenue; 804-355-8817; kubakuba.info; $-$$), a hole-in-the-wall cafe founded by a Cuban émigré, Manny Mendez. The brunch menu mixes paella and Cuban sandwiches with Huevos Kuba,

ABOVE AND OPPOSITE BELOW Jefferson Davis, gesturing grandly, and General J.E.B. Stuart, astride a cavalry horse, are among the sculpted Southern heroes on Monument Avenue. In the late 20th century this Confederate crowd was joined by a bronze of the tennis star Arthur Ashe.

eggs with Cuban-inflected hash, rice, and cornbread. Richmonders line up here for the straight-out-of-Havana vibe. The waitresses sway to Cuban music, and Kuba Kuba also doubles as a bodega where you can load up on Café Bustelo and Our Lady of Guadalupe candles.

11 *Art Factory* Noon

Once an industrial wasteland, the Manchester neighborhood has emerged as an arts district with loft apartments. The anchor is the former MeadWestvaco packaging plant, now a huge art complex with 75 studios and three galleries. Stroll through the mazelike **Art Works** (320 Hull Street; 804-291-1400; artworksrichmond.com), where artists sell their creations, many for under $200. Then, since you're in the neighborhood, head to **Legend Brewery** (321 West Seventh Street; 804-232-3446; legendbrewing.com; $), for a snack and a local microbrew.

ABOVE Bygones, a retro-inspired store in Carytown, a strip of shops and cafes frequented by an eclectic crowd.

OPPOSITE Sipping in style at afternoon tea in the elegantly appointed Jefferson Hotel.

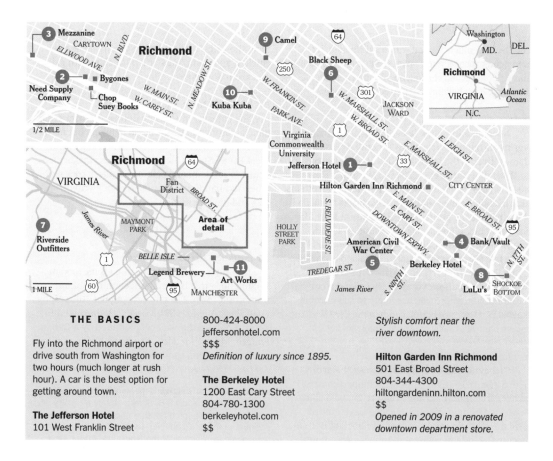

THE BASICS

Fly into the Richmond airport or drive south from Washington for two hours (much longer at rush hour). A car is the best option for getting around town.

The Jefferson Hotel
101 West Franklin Street

800-424-8000
jeffersonhotel.com
$$$
Definition of luxury since 1895.

The Berkeley Hotel
1200 East Cary Street
804-780-1300
berkeleyhotel.com
$$

Stylish comfort near the river downtown.

Hilton Garden Inn Richmond
501 East Broad Street
804-344-4300
hiltongardeninn.hilton.com
$$
Opened in 2009 in a renovated downtown department store.

Charlottesville

As far as Charlottesville is concerned, Thomas Jefferson might still be living on the hill at Monticello. There and at the University of Virginia, which he founded in 1819, he is referred to as "Mr. Jefferson" with a familiarity that suggests he might stroll past, horticulture manual in hand, at any moment. To this day an inordinate number of houses and buildings in the area resemble the back of a nickel. But Jefferson was always at the cutting edge, and the traveler today can share in some of that spirit, too, thanks to the energy emanating from the university he left behind. The active music scene has produced megastars like the Dave Matthews Band and helped to launch the modern roots-rock wave. Local chefs marry grits and fried chicken with international influences. Prize-winning vineyards checker the foothills, a development that Jefferson would have appreciated. He succeeded at nearly everything, but he couldn't coax a decent wine out of Virginia's soil.
— BY JENNIFER TUNG AND JOSHUA KURLANTZICK

FRIDAY

1 *Al Fresco Downtown* 5 p.m.

Walk through the oak-lined downtown mall, where students talk philosophy over coffee and locals gravitate for drinks. You will pass rows of restored brick buildings, street entertainers like mimes and violinists, a central plaza for public art, and al fresco cafes. Stop in just off the main mall at **Feast** (416 West Main Street, Suite H; 434-244-7800; feastvirginia.com), an artisanal cheese shop, charcuterie, and gourmet market that feels as if it could be in Paris.

2 *Old and New* 7 p.m.

Only 10 minutes from downtown Charlottesville, the **Clifton Inn** (1296 Clifton Inn Drive; 434-971-1800; cliftoninn.net; $$$$) sits amid rolling hills and pasture land. Virginia's inns have embarked on a culinary arms race, and the Clifton has kept up. Its restaurant, inside a white-pillared *Gone With*

OPPOSITE Monticello, Thomas Jefferson's home and a conspicuous example of his architectural prowess.

RIGHT The restaurant at the *Gone with the Wind*-style Clifton Inn is worth the drive out of town.

the Wind-style Southern mansion, offers a design-your-own tasting menu featuring local ingredients. Reservations are essential. For a more casual dinner, eat in Charlottesville at **C & O** (515 East Water Street; 434-971-7044; candorestaurant.com; $$-$$$), a 110-year-old building that originally served as a railroad stop. Sit in the mezzanine, a candlelit room as dark and narrow as a mine shaft, and order dishes like local organic lamb or house-made chorizo with braised collard greens and purple potato frites.

SATURDAY

3 *The Morning Tour* 8 a.m.

A quiet Saturday morning is a good time to see Jefferson's Academical Village, the central buildings he designed at the University of Virginia. Pick up coffee at **Mudhouse** on the Main Street mall (213 Main Street; 434-984-6833; mudhouse.com), and walk onto the Grounds (Mr. Jefferson never used the word "campus," and neither does anyone else in Charlottesville). Begin at the **Rotunda** (tours, 434-924-7969; virginia.edu/uvatours/rotunda), inspired by the Pantheon in Rome, which sits at the north end of the 225-foot-long Lawn. Flanking the Lawn are the Pavilions, where esteemed professors live, and dorm rooms occupied by high-achieving final-year students ("senior" isn't a word here,

either). The charming gardens behind the Pavilions, divided by undulating serpentine walls, are the professors' backyards but are open to the public.

4 *Outback* 10 a.m.

For a fascinating detour little known by outsiders, visit the university's **Kluge-Ruhe Aboriginal Art Collection**. John W. Kluge, a billionaire businessman, built perhaps the largest collection of aboriginal art outside Australia and then donated it to the University of Virginia. The free guided tour, every Saturday at 10:30 a.m., is essential to understanding these stark and sometimes inscrutable works of art (400 Worrell Drive, Peter Jefferson Place; 434-244-0234; virginia.edu/kluge-ruhe).

5 *Colonial Fried Chicken* Noon

Let the lady in the bonnet and the big skirt corral you into the lunch line at **Michie Tavern**, an inn that dates back to 1784 (683 Thomas Jefferson Parkway; 434-977-1234; michietavern.com; $$$). Let more women in bonnets pile fried chicken, black-eyed

BELOW Tasting at Barboursville Vineyard. The winery has a notable restaurant and a Jefferson-designed building.

OPPOSITE Comestibles at Feast, a stop on the oak-lined downtown mall near the University of Virginia.

peas, stewed tomatoes, and cornbread onto your pewter-style plate; then eat at a wooden table by the hearth. Once you accept full tourist status, the food is very tasty.

6 *The Back of the Nickel* 1 p.m.

Tours of historical sites are rarely billed as exciting, but Jefferson's home, **Monticello** (434-984-9800; monticello.org), actually causes goose bumps. Jefferson designed the house to invoke classical ideals of reason, proportion, and balance, and sited it on a rise ("Monticello" is from the Italian for "small hill") for a view of distant mountains. After your introduction at the new visitor center, opened in 2009, enter the house and note the elk antlers in the entrance hall, courtesy of Lewis and Clark, and the private library that once housed 6,700 books. Guides point out Jefferson's design innovations, including a dumbwaiter hidden in a fireplace, and offer insight into the unsung lives of the slaves who kept everything going. Monticello lost its spot on the back of the nickel coin for a brief period a few years ago, but Eric Cantor, a Virginia representative and influential House Republican, ushered through legislation to guarantee that after 2006 it would be back to stay.

7 *Country Roads* 5 p.m.

Drive back toward Charlottesville and turn northeast on Route 20 to Barboursville. The drive, through an area called the **Southwest Mountains Rural Historic District**, winds up and down through green farmland sitting in the shadow of the Southwest range. Keep your eyes out for historical marker signs; the area also boasts a rich trove of African-American history (nps.gov/history/nr/travel/journey/sou.htm).

8 *Dining Amid the Ruins* 7 p.m.

There's more of Jefferson (didn't this man ever sleep?) to be seen at the Barboursville Vineyard, where you should have made reservations well before now for dinner at the **Palladio Restaurant** (17655 Winery Road, Barboursville; 540-832-7848; barboursvillewine.net; $$$$). Jefferson designed the main building at the vineyard, which dates back to 1814. There was a fire in the late 1880s, but you can see the ruins of his design. The restaurant

features Northern Italian cooking as well as locally inspired dishes like quail with corn cakes.

9 *Miller Time* 10 p.m.

Every college town needs a few decent bars for grungy bands to play in, but in Charlottesville, you wind up later seeing those bands on MTV. The Dave Matthews Band had its start here back when Matthews tended bar at **Miller's** (109 West Main Street; 434-971-8511; millersdowntown.com). He moved on, but Miller's, a converted drugstore that retains the trappings of an old-time apothecary, is still there. Get there by 10, before the college crowd packs the place, and try to catch the one night of the week when the famed bebop jazz trumpeter and local music professor John D'earth headlines the bill.

SUNDAY

10 *Take a Hike* 10 a.m.

Drive west for 30 minutes on Interstate 64 to **Shenandoah National Park** (Exit 99). By mid-morning the early mist will have lifted. Follow signs to Skyline Drive and the Blue Ridge Parkway. For a vigorous hike, start at the Humpback Gap parking area, six miles south of the Blue Ridge Parkway's northern end. Follow the Appalachian Trail a half-mile south to a challenging spur trail that leads to a breathtaking view of the Shenandoah Valley.

THE BASICS

Drive about an hour northwest from Richmond or fly into the Charlottesville-Albermarle Airport. Explore the area by car.

Clifton Inn
1296 Clifton Inn Drive
434-971-1800
cliftoninn.net
$$$
Eighteen rooms and suites on a 100-acre property with walking trails, tennis, and a pool.

200 South Street Inn
200 South Street West
434-979-0200
southstreetinn.com
$$
Inn in a stately mansion in the center of town.

Omni Charlottesville
235 Main Street
434-971-5500
omnihotels.com
$$$
Well-appointed 208-room downtown hotel.

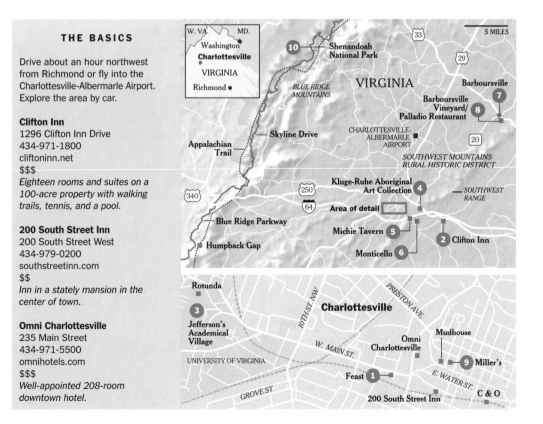

Williamsburg

Williamsburg, Virginia, with its restored Historic Area of 18th-century buildings, will always be a destination for education-minded families, Revolutionary War buffs, and anyone who likes to imagine life in another time. But Williamsburg can also be a more rounded—and upscale—experience. Local chefs have updated traditional Southern cooking, and the food is often accompanied by high-quality Virginia wines. Among the Colonial homes of Williamsburg's central district, it's possible to have a spa treatment or buy interesting folk art. Of course if you want to see a staging of Patrick Henry's "Give Me Liberty, or Give Me Death!" speech, or stick your head in the stocks, that's still there, too.

— BY JOSHUA KURLANTZICK

FRIDAY

1 *Virginia Vintages* 4 p.m.

Once consigned to the bargain bin of wine shops, Virginia wines now hold their own in global wine competitions, and the **Williamsburg Winery**, a few miles from the colonial district (5800 Wessex Hundred Road; 757-229-0999; williamsburgwinery.com), is one of the largest in the state. Its chardonnays—particularly the fruity, oaky Acte 12 chardonnay—have won much acclaim from critics. Attend a tasting and then head over to the adjacent tavern for a light pre-dinner snack.

2 *Barbecue and Pound Cake* 7 p.m.

Southerners can argue about barbecue with the same spirit they exhibit for college football, and Virginia-style barbecue is certainly worthy of a heated debate. It tends to be smokier and milder than North Carolina's vinegary, tangy version. In the Williamsburg area, **Pierce's Pitt Bar-B-Que** (447 East Rochambeau Drive; 757-565-2955; pierces.com; $$) is a local legend. The smell of smoking meat wafts out of the restaurant and even pervades a nearby stretch of highway. At all times of the day, the parking lot is packed and crowds clamber for barbecue sandwiches and full racks of ribs. Pork rules, but Pierce's also serves chicken, salads, buttery corn bread, and

homemade carrot and lemon pound cakes. (But beware: if you ask for a chicken salad, the waiter may think there's something wrong with you.)

3 *The Neighborhood* 8:30 p.m.

Most visitors to Williamsburg stay in hotels outside the **Historic Area**, but by far the most interesting (though largely unknown) lodging option is to stay in a restored home, tavern, or other structure within the colonial district. Whether or not you're unpacking your suitcase right in the neighborhood, after dinner take a leisurely stroll through the heart of the district, dead quiet once all the tourists have left.

SATURDAY

4 *Back in Time* 10 a.m.

It's best to check out the Colonial buildings and re-enactments in the morning, before the heat and humidity and tourist buses arrive. *Colonial Williamsburg This Week*, a free print publication, contains up-to-date listings of re-enactments, but don't miss the **Governor's Palace**, home to royal governors (and Patrick Henry) and the **Bruton Parish Church** (one of the oldest Episcopal churches in America). And look for re-enactors who are engaged in political debates, which tend to be less stilted than other re-enactments.

OPPOSITE The Wythe House, one of the 18th-century buildings of Williamsburg, a restored colonial-era city.

RIGHT A craft shop at Merchants Square.

5 *The People's Art* Noon

Abby Aldrich Rockefeller was one of the earliest patrons of American folk art, and her collection, housed in the **Abby Aldrich Rockefeller Folk Art Museum** (325 West Francis Street; history.org/history/museums) showcases the immense diversity of the genre. The collection ranges from staid family portraits to whimsical sculptures of watermelons to elegiac paintings of Christ that resemble the works of El Greco. Because folk art is less known than, say, Picasso's, take a docent-guided tour of the collection.

6 *Merchants of Americana* 2 p.m.

More than just a purveyor of cider mugs and souvenir tricorner hats, **Merchants Square**, on the west end of the Colonial District, also serves up unusual—and often pricey—antiques, quilts, silver, and other American crafts. Try the **Nancy Thomas Gallery of Folk Art** (402 West Duke of Gloucester Street; 757-259-1938; nancythomas.com) or **J. Fenton Modern American Crafts** (110 South Henry Street; 757-221-8200; quiltsunlimited.com) for updated interpretations—in jewelry, clothing, and other formats—of the quirky traditions of folk art found in the Rockefeller collection. For lunch, grab a sandwich at the **Cheese Shop** (410 West Duke of Gloucester Street; 757-220-1324; cheeseshopwilliamsburg.com) on the square.

7 *Old-Time Pampering* 5 p.m.

Exhausted from a long day of walking and shopping? A visit to the **Spa of Colonial Williamsburg** (307 South England Street; 800-688-6479; colonialwilliamsburgresort.com/spa) might just be what you need. Right in the Historic Area, the spa serves the usual menu of treatments, but in keeping with the history theme, it also offers a twist: packages based on practices from the early days of American history—for example, an 18th-century treatment with colonial-era herbs like pennyroyal, sage, rosemary, angelica, and juniper berries.

8 *Dinner Update* 7 p.m.

Situated right on Merchants Square, **Fat Canary** (410 West Duke of Gloucester Street; 757-229-3333; fatcanarywilliamsburg.com; $$$) quickly established itself with a departure from the pub-style food and alehouse atmosphere more typical in the heart of Colonial Williamsburg. In a well-designed, Art Deco-influenced dining area, Fat Canary serves nouvelle cuisine that gives local dishes innovative treatment, resulting in combinations like crispy cornmeal oysters with charred tomato or free-range pheasant with polenta, pine nuts, and pancetta. Reservations are essential.

SUNDAY

9 *Take a Drive* 9 a.m.

If you have children along, this is a good day to indulge them with a side trip to the **Busch Gardens** theme park, just three miles east of Williamsburg. But for something more serene, take a drive. You have to go only a few miles outside Colonial Williamsburg, past the mall sprawl, to appreciate the rural character of much of the surrounding area. Head onto the 23-mile-long **Colonial Parkway**, a winding, wooded

ABOVE See the Colonial-era buildings and re-enactments in the morning, before the heat and tourist buses arrive.

BELOW One interesting lodging option is a stay in a restored home, tavern, or other structure.

road connecting three Virginia towns important in history: Williamsburg, Jamestown, and Yorktown. With a low speed limit, it's perfect for a mellow tour, stopping at scenic turnouts to look out at the York and James Rivers.

10 *Bottoms Up* Noon

In colonial times, Williamsburg was known as much for drinking as for debating. Taverns served as meeting places, the perfect setting for wielding influence in the powerful Virginia colony. The restored Historic Area features four working taverns—all serving lunch, dinner, or both—striving to recreate an authentic atmosphere. Most feature workaday fare like sandwiches and local seafood, but the ambience

can't be beat. Try **Chowning's Tavern** (109 East Duke of Gloucester Street; 757-229-2141; $$) for lunch. Its garden tables offer views of Market Square and the Governor's Palace (it does not take reservations). After lunch, it's an easy walk to the lavish **Peyton Randolph House** and other central Colonial homes.

ABOVE At Pierce's Pitt Bar-B-Que, the meat is cooked Virginia-style and the parking lot is always packed. Pork is king, but savor the buttery cornbread, too.

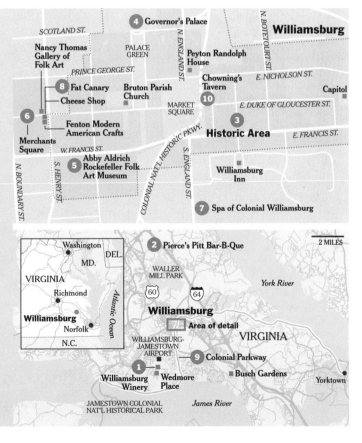

THE BASICS

Fly into Norfolk or Richmond, Virginia, or drive three to four hours from Washington.

You'll need a car for exploring.

Colonial Houses — Historic Lodging
Williamsburg Historic Area
800-447-8679
history.org
$$
Lodging in houses within the Historic Area; a good first-visit experience, especially with children.

Williamsburg Inn
136 East Francis Street
800-447-8679
colonialwilliamsburgresort.com
$$$$
Built in 1937, a National Trust Historic Hotel with indoor pool and modern comforts.

Wedmore Place
5810 Wessex Hundred
757-941-0310
wedmoreplace.com
$$
At the Williamsburg Winery, newly built in Colonial style.

Map labels:
Governor's Palace
Williamsburg
SCOTLAND ST.
Nancy Thomas Gallery of Folk Art
PALACE GREEN
Peyton Randolph House
N. BOTETOURT ST.
N. ENGLAND ST.
PRINCE GEORGE ST.
Chowning's Tavern
E. NICHOLSON ST.
8 Fat Canary
Bruton Parish Church
Capitol
Cheese Shop
MARKET SQUARE
E. DUKE OF GLOUCESTER ST.
6
Fenton Modern American Crafts
Merchants Square
W. FRANCIS ST.
Historic Area
E. FRANCIS ST.
N. BOUNDARY ST.
S. HENRY ST.
5 Abby Aldrich Rockefeller Folk Art Museum
COLONIAL NAT'L HISTORIC PKWY.
S. ENGLAND ST.
Williamsburg Inn
7 Spa of Colonial Williamsburg
Washington
DEL.
MD.
2 Pierce's Pitt Bar-B-Que
2 MILES
WALLER MILL PARK
York River
VIRGINIA
Richmond
60
64
Williamsburg
Williamsburg
Norfolk
Area of detail
N.C.
WILLIAMSBURG-JAMESTOWN AIRPORT
VIRGINIA
9 Colonial Parkway
Busch Gardens
Yorktown
Williamsburg Winery
Wedmore Place
Atlantic Ocean
JAMESTOWN COLONIAL NAT'L HISTORICAL PARK
James River

Virginia Beach

In 1607, a group of adventurers landed at Cape Henry, now known as Virginia Beach, but moved on to Jamestown to establish England's first permanent American colony. Four centuries later, Virginia Beach isn't snubbed anymore. It's the largest city in Virginia, home to more than 440,000 people and part of a metropolitan area of 1.6 million that also includes Norfolk and Newport News. Famous for its naval installations and picturesque shorelines, Virginia Beach also has an array of famous residents past and present: the hip-hop stars Missy Elliott, Tim Mosley (a k a Timbaland), and Chad Hugo and Pharrell Williams; the televangelist Pat Robertson; and the legendary psychic Edgar Cayce, who in 1925 was "called" to live in this city, with its gentle climate and lush locale along the Atlantic shore.
— BY LISA RICHMON

FRIDAY

1 *Kiss Off* 4 p.m.

Perch across the street from the Naval Air Station Oceana for a chance to see what the Navy's top fighter jocks are doing with your tax dollars. Look for takeoffs, landings, and — if you're lucky — more. After maneuvers over the ocean, pilots turn their F/A-18 Hornets and Super Hornets back to the base in formation. The lead pilot gives the "kiss off," the signal to peel off and land, and the planes simulate a carrier landing by dropping sharply onto a box painted on the runway. Watch for it from the jet landing observation area at **POW/MIA Flame of Hope Memorial Park** (Oceana Boulevard near the intersection with Bells Road).

2 *Virginia Is for Beach Lovers* 5 p.m.

Virginia Beach is all about its boardwalk, fringed with flowers and outdoor cafes, and its 100-yard-wide beach. Catch the sea breeze and look around. You will see joyful children, preening sun-bathers, and surfer dudes. Each August competitors arrive here for the East Coast Surfing Championship. Fishermen find a second home at the central pier off 15th Street.

OPPOSITE Sand, boardwalk, and city at Virginia Beach.

RIGHT The breakfast menu at Doc Taylor's includes the Heart Attack: eggs with sausage, bacon, and steak.

3 *New Southern Cooking* 7 p.m.

Sushi parlors have sprouted up where once there was only Virginia ham, and the hands-down favorite is **Mizuno Japanese Restaurant** (1860 Laskin Road; 757-422-1200; mizuno-sushi.com; $$), run by Walter Mizuno, a sushi chef born and trained in Tokyo. Look for the tuna tartare and the delicately loaded sashimi salad of octopus, avocado, tuna, seaweed, and fresh greens. For accompaniment, Mizuno offers the largest sake list in the area.

SATURDAY

4 *Magic Morning* 6:30 a.m.

A due east sunrise that lights up the boardwalk from 1st Street to 40th Street is what locals love most about Virginia Beach. The rich coastline means good feeding for dolphins that pop up from the ocean and pelicans that glide along the air current of a wave for miles. Large ships dot the seascape, and broken crockery from centuries-old shipwrecks still washes up on shore.

5 *Sample and Shop* 9 a.m.

Nibble breakfast and pick up picnic food for later at the **Old Beach Farmers Market** (620 19th Street; oldbeachfarmersmarket.com) in the parking lot of Crocs eco-bistro. You will find fresh fruit in season, baked goods, Virginia artisanal cheeses, and boutique organic wines. Then shop for beachwear at the **17th Street Surf Shop** (1612 Pacific Avenue; 757-422-6105; 17thstsurfshop.com), where surfers find denims for their dry off-hours, or at **Meg's Swimwear** (307 Laskin Road; 757-428-7945), known for fitting

swimsuits to women's bodies rather than expecting things to work the other way around.

6 *Where Ocean Meets Bay* Noon

First Landing State Park (2500 Shore Drive; 757-412-2300; dcr.virginia.gov/state_parks/fir.shtml) commemorates the spot where the settlers of 1607 established an elective government before pushing on to Jamestown. Today, it's the most visited park in Virginia, a nearly 3,000-acre paradise for cyclists, hikers, and nature lovers, at the spot where the Atlantic Ocean meets the Chesapeake Bay. Hike some of the nine walking trails, totaling 19 miles, that wind around dunes and ponds surrounded by moss-covered live oak and bald cypress trees.

7 *Aura of Health* 3 p.m.

Edgar Cayce was a farm boy from Kentucky who harnessed his psychic powers to "enter" other people's bodies to diagnose illnesses, which he then treated with what he called readings. He also made general predictions of the future (reportedly he foresaw the stock market crash and World War II) and gained the attention of scientists, medical experts, and President Woodrow Wilson. In 1925 Cayce settled

ABOVE Joyous children, preening sun-bathers, fishermen, and surfer dudes populate the beach. Overhead, fighter jets streak toward Naval Air Station Oceana.

in Virginia Beach and in 1928 he founded the Cayce Hospital, based on his faith-healing principles. It closed two years later, but at the **Association for Research and Enlightenment**, dedicated to Cayce's legacy (215 67th Street, Virginia Beach; 757-428-3588; edgarcayce.org), you can browse the gift shop, buy holistic products, and attend a day spa offering Cayce-based remedies dispensed with the belief that we are all just one session of colon hydrotherapy away from attaining good chi.

8 *Catch of the Night* 7 p.m.

For a great view of the scenery of both the natural and Saturday-night varieties, hit **Catch 31 Fish House and Bar** at the **Hilton Virginia Beach Oceanfront** (3001 Atlantic Avenue, 757-213-3474; catch31.com; $$$). The large glass bar extends outdoors, where it overlooks the boardwalk. Inside, the jam-packed grazing area is flanked by two dining areas offering a large selection of fresh fish. A raw bar features several varieties of oysters.

9 *Reggae Meets Rugelach* 9 p.m.

The **Jewish Mother** (Laskin and First Colonial Roads; 757-622-5915; jewishmother.com) is a deli by day and a restaurant and live-music bar by night. John Hammond, Roomful of Blues, and Dr. John are among the performers who have appeared on its stage; local bands play four or five nights a week.

If you're hungry, the Mother's Son Reuben is a specialty of the house, as is, of course, the chicken soup with matzo balls.

SUNDAY

10 *Eggs on the Veranda* 9 a.m.

In 1949, before Virginia Beach had a proper hospital, there was **Doc Taylor's** home office. Today, it's an all-day breakfast and lunch joint (207 23rd Street; 757-425-1960; doctaylors.com; $-$$), and the big doses of sunlight that pour into its covered porch are just what the doctor ordered. Breakfasts at Doc Taylor's include the Heart Attack (three eggs, bacon, and a strip steak) and the Nurse Ratchett (omelet

with grilled red peppers, portobellos, spinach, and hollandaise). **Tautog's**, the sister cottage next door (No. 205; 757-422-0081; tautogs.com; $$), takes over when Doc Taylor's closes at 5 p.m.

11 *Sea and Be Seen* 11 a.m.

The **Virginia Aquarium and Marine Science Center** (717 General Booth Boulevard; 757-425-3474; virginiaaquarium.com) features a 300,000-gallon tank with sharks and stingrays, a 100,000-gallon Red Sea Aquarium tank, an adjacent salt marsh and woodland preserve, and an IMAX theater. Dolphin-watching tours, led by the center's knowledgeable staff, run daily in summer and on weekends into October (757-437-2628 for reservations).

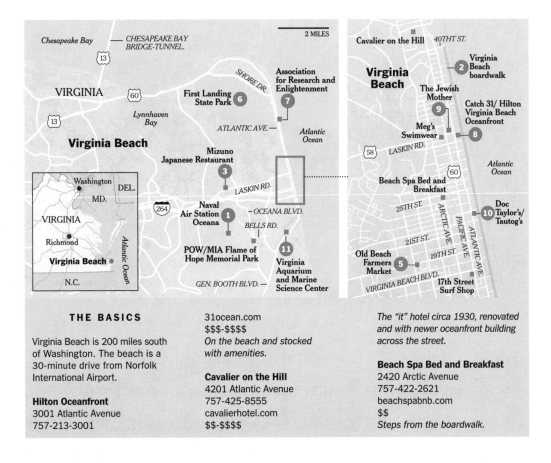

THE BASICS

Virginia Beach is 200 miles south of Washington. The beach is a 30-minute drive from Norfolk International Airport.

Hilton Oceanfront
3001 Atlantic Avenue
757-213-3001

31ocean.com
$$$-$$$$
On the beach and stocked with amenities.

Cavalier on the Hill
4201 Atlantic Avenue
757-425-8555
cavalierhotel.com
$$-$$$$

The "it" hotel circa 1930, renovated and with newer oceanfront building across the street.

Beach Spa Bed and Breakfast
2420 Arctic Avenue
757-422-2621
beachspabnb.com
$$
Steps from the boardwalk.

Raleigh-Durham

Tell North Carolinians you're heading to the Raleigh-Durham area, locally called the Research Triangle or just the Triangle, and they will probably ask, "Which school are you visiting?" Yet the close-knit cities of Raleigh, Durham, and Chapel Hill, North Carolina, are marked by more than college bars and basketball fans. Visitors not bound for Duke (Durham), the University of North Carolina (Chapel Hill), or North Carolina State (Raleigh) come to see buzz-worthy bands, dine on food from farm-worshiping chefs, and explore outdoor art. From its biscuits to its boutiques, the Triangle occupies a happy place between slow-paced Southern charm and urban cool.
— BY J. J. GOODE

FRIDAY

1 *Art Inside Out* 3 p.m.

The collection at the **North Carolina Museum of Art** (2110 Blue Ridge Road, Raleigh; 919-839-6262; ncartmuseum.org) is succinct by major museum standards, and that has its advantages. The lack of tour bus crowds means unfettered access to the museum's Old Masters and contemporary heavyweights like Anselm Kiefer. The real treat is the adjacent Museum Park, more than 164 acres of open fields and woodlands punctuated by environmental art like Cloud Chamber, a stone hut that acts as a camera obscura with a small hole in the roof projecting inverted, otherworldly images of slowly swaying trees on the floor and walls.

2 *Tower of Bauble* 5 p.m.

There's no pigeonholing the eclectic wares in the four-story indie mini-mall collectively known as **Father & Son Antiques** (107 West Hargett Street, Raleigh; 919-832-3030; swankarama.com) and including Southern Swank and 2nd Floor Vintage. The organizing principle, if there is one, might be high design meets kitschy Americana, as the intermingling of vintage disco dresses, Mexican wrestling masks, and Eames aluminum chairs attests.

3 *Upscale Diner* 7 p.m.

Memorable meals abound in the Triangle owing to its high concentration of accomplished, produce-fondling chefs like Ashley Christensen.

She left one of the area's top kitchens to open **Poole's Downtown Diner** (426 South McDowell Street, Raleigh; 919-832-4477; poolesdowntowndiner.com; $-$$) in a space that began as a 1940s pie shop. Diners sitting in the bright-red booths dig into Christensen's low-pretense, high-flavor dishes. You might find a starter of lovably sloppy fried green tomatoes crowned with local pork smoked over cherry wood, or an entree of ground-in-house chuck roll seared in duck fat, topped with cheese, and perched on a slice of grilled brioche.

4 *Cheers to the Chief* 10 p.m.

The owner of the **Raleigh Times Bar** (14 East Hargett Street, Raleigh; 919-833-0999; raleightimesbar.com), Greg Hatem, painstakingly restored the century-old building that once housed the now-defunct *Raleigh Times* and decorated the walls with old clippings, paperboy bags, and other artifacts from the newspaper's heyday. The place was soon packed with patrons choosing from more than 100 beers, including esoteric Belgians and local brews you won't find elsewhere. Barack Obama showed up the day of the state's Democratic primary in 2008, bought a $2 Pabst Blue Ribbon, and left an $18 tip. Anyone not campaigning might make a pricier selection.

OPPOSITE Outdoor entertainment at the Koka Booth Amphitheatre in Cary, a Raleigh suburb.

BELOW Biscuit aficionados find drive-through nirvana at Sunrise Biscuit Kitchen.

SATURDAY

5 *Eco Junk* 10:30 a.m.

The **Scrap Exchange** (548 Foster Street, Durham; 919-688-6960; scrapexchange.org) is a "nonprofit creative reuse center" specializing in industrial discards or, for those not versed in eco-jargon, a bazaar of modestly priced former junk donated by Carolinians and scavenged from local businesses that have included a hosiery mill, a zipper factory, and a parachute plant. Even if you are not one of the giddy artists, teachers, or theater producers who comb for utilitarian treasures, plan to spend at least an hour rummaging in a cool-struck trance through items like test tubes, empty fire extinguishers, and swaths of double-knit polyester.

6 *Taco Time* Noon

Anyone not on a hunt for serious Mexican food might drive past **Taqueria La Vaquita** (2700 Chapel Hill Road, Durham; 919-402-0209; lavaquitanc.com; $), an unassuming freestanding structure with a plastic cow on its roof, just five minutes from Duke University. But if you did, you'd miss tacos made with house-made corn tortillas, uncommonly delicate discs topped with exceptional barbacoa de res (slow-cooked beef) or carnitas (braised-then-fried pork).

7 *River Walk* 2 p.m.

One of the Triangle's charms is that its urban trappings and booming suburbs, like upscale Cary, are so easy to escape. A 10-mile drive from downtown Durham brings you to **Eno River State Park** (6101 Cole Mill Road, Durham; 919-383-1686; ncparks.gov). Its trails progress through swaying pines and follow the river past patches of delicate purple-and-yellow wildflowers and turtles sunning themselves on low branches in the water.

ABOVE University of North Carolina basketball fans. The excitement rises when the opponent is Duke University.

RIGHT High design meets Americana kitsch at Father & Son Antiques in Raleigh, an eclectic four-story mini-mall.

8 *Going for the Whole Hog* 5 p.m.

Small towns and back roads, not cities, have a monopoly on great barbecue. What makes **The Pit** (328 West Davie Street, Raleigh; 919-890-4500; thepit-raleigh.com; $) a striking exception is Ed Mitchell, the legendary master of the eastern North Carolina art form of whole hog cooking. Instead of trekking 100 miles to porcine capitals like Ayden and Lexington, you can dig into pilgrimage-worthy chopped or pulled pork—made from pigs purchased from family farms and cooked for 10 to 14 hours over coals and hickory or oak—just a short stroll from the North Carolina Capitol Building. Your chopped barbecued pork plate comes with two sides and greaseless hush puppies.

9 *Root for the Home Team* 7 p.m.

The Triangle is college basketball country, home to two of the winningest teams—Duke and North Carolina—and some of the most rabid fans in college sports history. But soon after the madness of March, the more tranquil fans of local baseball stream into the **Durham Bulls Athletic Park** (409 Blackwell Street, Durham; 919-687-6500; dbulls.com). The Bulls, founded in 1902 as the Tobacconists, still offer professional baseball at bargain prices.

10 *Big Bands* 10 p.m.

Nirvana played at the **Cat's Cradle** (300 East Main Street, Carrboro; 919-967-9053; catscradle.com) for the first time in pre-*Nevermind* 1990 to about 100 people. A year later Pearl Jam played to three times as many, filling just half the standing-room-only space. Today the Cradle, just a mile from downtown

BELOW When college basketball ends, it's time for local baseball fans to stream into Durham Bulls Athletic Park. Professional baseball in Durham dates back to 1902.

Chapel Hill, hosts acts you may be hearing more about tomorrow, for low ticket prices that seem more like yesterday.

SUNDAY

11 *Drive-Thru Biscuits* 10 a.m.

There are several places in Chapel Hill that serve a distinguished Southern breakfast for an easy-to-swallow price. Diners linger over gravy-smothered pork chops and eggs at **Mama Dip's** (408 West Rosemary Street; 919-942-5837; mamadips.com) and

peerless shrimp and grits at **Crook's Corner** (610 West Franklin Street; 919-929-7643; crookscorner.com). But for a morning meal on the go that's equally unforgettable, roll up to the drive-through-only **Sunrise Biscuit Kitchen** (1305 East Franklin Street; 919-933-1324; $), where the iced tea is tooth-achingly sweet and the main course is fluffy, buttery, and filled with salty country ham or crisp fried chicken.

ABOVE Museum Park is 164 acres of woodland, grassy fields, and outdoor artworks adjacent to the Carolina Museum of Art in Raleigh.

OPPOSITE A trail system at Museum Park allows for art viewing simultaneously with jogging, hiking, or bicycling. Many trails lead to commissioned works.

THE BASICS

The Triangle is easily accessible on interstate highways. Or fly into Raleigh-Durham International Airport and rent a car.

Umstead Hotel and Spa
5 SAS Campus Drive, Cary
866-877-4141
theumstead.com
$$$-$$$$
About 15 minutes from downtown Raleigh, with pool and spa.

Arrowhead Inn
106 Mason Road, Durham
919-477-8430
arrowheadinn.com
$$
Rooms, garden cottage, and log cabin amid lawns and magnolia trees.

Carolina Inn
211 Pittsboro Street, Chapel Hill
800-962-8519
carolinainn.com
$$
Southern grandeur on the University of North Carolina campus.

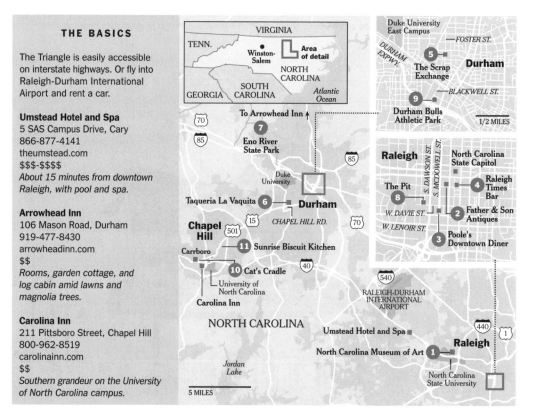

Charleston

Charleston, South Carolina, still has its cannons aimed at Fort Sumter, where the Civil War began. With some of the country's most aggressive historic preservation, it maintains magnolia-and-hibiscus charm on streets lined with Colonial and antebellum mansions. Tours give visitors a glimpse of the lives and language of the African-American people who built the Gullah culture nearby. But a newer and younger Charleston asserts itself, too—in galleries on Broad Street and in a festoonery of restaurants, bars, and boutique bakeries in the design district on upper King Street. Charlestonians, governed by laws of hospitality as incontrovertible as those of gravity, cannot help themselves from sharing their new finds, even if you are "from off," as those who grew up on this once swampy peninsula refer to outsiders.
— BY SHAILA DEWAN

FRIDAY

1 *Meeting Lucinda* 3 p.m.

Embracing the past doesn't always mean being honest about it, but the new Charleston acknowledges both sides of its history. The four-block **Gateway Walk** shares hidden beauty, taking visitors through quiet gardens and past lovely old churches. Enter it from Church Street across from St. Philip's Episcopal Church, and follow the plaques. Next, walk a couple of blocks to see the darker past. In 1856, the city banned outdoor slave markets as out of keeping with its genteel image. Trade moved indoors to places like Ryan's Mart, where the first sale was a 20-year-old woman named Lucinda. The building opened in 2007 as the **Old Slave Mart Museum** (6 Chalmers Street; 843-958-6467; nps.gov/history/nr/travel/charleston). It brings slavery to horrifying life, addressing topics like the stigma attached to slave trading and the ways slaves were dressed, shaved, and fed in preparation for market day.

2 *Lowcountry Cuisine* 7 p.m.

Charleston is the unofficial capital of the swampy coastal Lowcountry in this part of South Carolina. For a taste of its traditional cuisine gone upscale, have dinner at **Cypress Lowcountry Grille** (167 East Bay Street, 843-727-0111; magnolias-blossom-cypress.com; $$$), where the chef, Craig Deihl, makes his own charcuterie

(served with lard biscuits) and pork schnitzel while throwing a bone to value-seeking diners with a prix fixe menu for about $40.

3 *Jazz Refuge* 10 p.m.

Charleston is not particularly known for its night life—the options sometimes come down to one outlandishly named martini versus another (caramel macchiatotini? Charlestoniantini?). But locals with an evening to kill stop by the lounge of the Charleston Grill, a grand ballroom of a restaurant tucked away in a posh hotel, the **Charleston Place** (224 King Street; 843-577-4522; charlestongrill.com). From a glamorous white banquette, you can take in the sophisticated tunes of the Quentin Baxter Ensemble and the very polite antics of practically all of Charleston, from dads and debutantes to Gullah painters. Snack on truffle Parmesan popcorn and a kiwi version of the Pimm's cup.

SATURDAY

4 *Sweetgrass and Crepes* 9 a.m.

The old South finds new takes at the **Charleston Farmers Market** in Marion Square (843-724-7305; charlestonarts.sc), a bustling downtown market where you may find pickled watermelon rind, sweetgrass baskets, and flower arrangements that

OPPOSITE Guided kayaking tours take paddlers into the marshy terrain of South Carolina's Lowcountry.

BELOW Shopping at the Charleston Farmers Market.

make use of old windows. Be prepared to fight your way through the throngs buying their week's supply of groceries or lining up for fresh crepes (charlestoncrepecompany.com).

5 *Shopping Belles* 10 a.m.

King Street has long been the stylish epicenter of Charleston, but it's been invaded by the major chain stores. Take refuge on and around upper King, north of Marion Square, where chic shops and high-concept restaurants coexist with fading emporiums. Pick up a handy one-page guide to parking and neighborhood restaurants at **Blue Bicycle Books** (420 King Street; 843-722-2666; bluebicyclebooks.com). Sample a pastry at the fashionably French **Macaroon Boutique** (45 John Street; 843-577-5441; macaroonboutique.com), and then browse the baffling assortment of odds and ends at **Read Brothers**, established in 1912 (593 King Street; 843-723-7276; readbrothers.com), which now calls itself a stereo and fabric store. For a splurge, head to **Magar Hatworks** (57 Cannon Street; 843-345-4483; magarhatworks.com; call for appointment), a millinery where Leigh Magar makes recherché hats (around $175 to $700) that sell at high-end stores like Barneys New York.

6 *Not Quite Teetotaling* 2 p.m.

Many people spend a lifetime trying to replicate Grandma's recipes — not so at **Irvin-House Vineyards** (6775 Bears Bluff Road, 843-559-6867; charlestonwine.com), a scenic vineyard about a 30-minute drive from downtown on sleepy Wadmalaw Island. The owners have spent years trying to make muscadine wine without the syrupy, made-at-home sweetness those words bring to Southerners' minds. A few years ago, the owners took on another iconic Southern taste, iced tea,

ABOVE Leigh Magar, the milliner behind Magar Hatworks.

OPPOSITE Jazz at the Charleston Grill, tucked away in the posh Charleston Place hotel.

blending it with vodka to make Firefly Sweet Tea Vodka, whose authentic lazy-Sunday-afternoon flavor made it a runaway success. After the free Saturday vineyard tour at 2 p.m., you can taste both.

7 *Old Growth* 4 p.m.

On the way back to town, take a short detour to the **Angel Oak**, a tree so large it could whomp 10 Hogwarts willows (3688 Angel Oak Road). The tree, which is thought to be at least 300 to 400 years old, is threatened by plans for a nearby shopping center. It is protected by a fence; the gate closes at 5 p.m.

8 *Fish Camp Supper* 6 p.m.

Before the **Bowens Island Restaurant** burned down in 2006, the humble cinderblock fish camp was covered in decades' worth of graffiti scrawled by loyal customers. Eventually, it reopened in a large, screened-in room on 18-foot stilts, with a nicer deck and a better view of the dolphins playing in Folly Creek (1870 Bowens Island Road, 843-795-2757; bowensislandrestaurant.com; $$). Marker-wielding patrons have wasted no time in trying to cover the new lumber with fresh scrawls. You can try to decipher them as you wait for your roasted oysters and oversize hush puppies. Get here early to avoid the crush.

9 *Georgian Encore* 8 p.m.

When the **Dock Street Theater** (135 Church Street) opened in 1736, the first production had a name only a pre-Revolutionary could love: *The Recruiting Officer*. Luckily, the producers chose a different work, *Flora*, an early English opera, when it reopened in 2010 with all its Georgian splendor restored. Said to be the first building in America built to be a theater, the Dock hosts the Spoleto Festival, the city's artistic crown jewel, in May and June (spoletousa.org) and Charleston Stage (charlestonstage.com), which presents musicals and popular fare, the rest of the year.

SUNDAY

10 *Sticky and Delicious* 9 a.m.

When it opened, **WildFlour Pastry** (73 Spring Street, 843-327-2621; wildflourpastrycharleston.com) created an instant tradition with "sticky bun

Sundays." A steady stream of customers comes through the door in search of this warm, chewy, generously pecanned confection. Those with less of a sweet tooth will be happy with crumbly, fruity, or savory scones or a hardboiled Sea Island egg.

11 *Gardens and Gators* 11 a.m.

Ever since Pat Conroy's novel *Prince of Tides*, Charleston has been known for its mossy Lowcountry terrain as much as for its picturesque history. At **Middleton Place** plantation (4300 Ashley River Road; 800-782-3608; middletonplace.org), one of several plantations within easy reach of downtown, you can get a close-up view of the marsh — or, in winter, of a primeval cypress swamp — on a guided kayak tour. Alligators, bald eagles, and river otters are among the possible sights, as is the architectural award-winning **Inn at Middleton Place**, where the tours meet (4290 Ashley River Road; 843-628-2879; charlestonkayakcompany.blogspot.com). After your paddle, you can take in domesticated nature on the plantation grounds, billed as the oldest landscaped garden in the country, with twin butterfly lakes, or visit the blacksmith and cooper workshops. Some things in Charleston don't change.

THE BASICS

Multiple airlines fly to Charleston. Walk in the downtown. To explore further, rent a car.

Hampton Inn Charleston-Historic District
345 Meeting Street
843-723-4000
hamptoninn.hilton.com
$$
In a restored warehouse just old enough to be billed as the area's only antebellum hotel.

Battery Carriage House Inn
20 South Battery
843-727-3100
batterycarriagehouse.com
$$
Eleven rooms a stone's throw from White Point Gardens at the Battery. Enjoy breakfast in a shady walled garden reputed to be haunted.

Market Pavilion Hotel
225 East Bay Street
843-723-0500
marketpavilion.com
$$$$
Opulent rooms with mahogany furniture and four-poster beds.

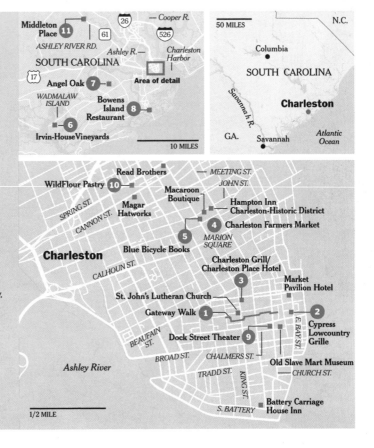

Savannah

Certain things about Savannah never change — it remains one of America's loveliest cities, organized around a grid of 21 squares, where children play, couples wed, and in the evenings lone saxophonists deliver a jazz soundtrack. Live oaks shade the squares; shops and cafes occupy stately old houses; ships still arrive on the Savannah River. But Savannah also has an appetite for the new. A growing emphasis on art has brought both a major expansion of the South's oldest art museum and a lively contemporary scene energized by students and instructors at the booming Savannah College of Art and Design. Civic boosters (thinking technology as well as art) are even trying to reposition the region as Georgia's Creative Coast. And then there is change of another kind: restoration. Before iron-clad protection of the historic district was established, Savannah lost 3 of its 24 squares to developers. Now one of the oldest, Ellis Square, long dominated by a parking lot, has been brought back with restored buildings on its edges and a statue of Savannah's favorite son, the songwriter Johnny Mercer, in its bright new center.

— BY SHAILA DEWAN

FRIDAY

1 *Good and Evil* 3:30 p.m.

You're in the heart of the gracious South, so embrace every cliché from the frilly to the Gothic, with some eccentric characters for good measure. Begin with a tour of the splendid **Mercer Williams House** on Monterey Square (430 Whitaker Street; 912-236-6352; mercerhouse.com; $12.50). It was built in the 1860s for Johnny Mercer's great-grandfather and restored by Jim Williams, the antiques dealer memorialized in a now-classic book, *Midnight in the Garden of Good and Evil*. The stern guide won't dwell on the three murder trials of Mr. Williams, who was acquitted, and guests aren't allowed on the second floor, where Mr. Williams's sister, Dorothy Kingery, still lives. But the guide will offer plenty of detail about the formal

OPPOSITE Savannah, Georgia, in the heart of the gracious South, carefully preserves the elegant houses lining its central grid of oak-shaded squares.

RIGHT The ornate cast-iron fountain in Forsyth Park.

courtyard, the nap-ready veranda, the Continental rococo, and the Edwardian Murano glass.

2 *Georgia on Your Plate* 7 p.m.

Dress up a bit (no flip-flops) for the froufrou milieu of **Elizabeth on 37th** (105 East 37th Street; 912-236-5547; elizabethon37th.net; $$$), a Lowcountry restaurant housed in an early 20th-century mansion where the décor may be prissy but the food is anything but. Expect a seafood-rich menu and what is arguably Savannah's quintessential dining experience. Look for Georgia shrimp, local sea bass, or a pecan crust on the rack of lamb. A seven-course tasting menu is $90 a person.

3 *Creepy Cocktails* 9 p.m.

The city of Savannah began peacefully enough, with a friendship between Tomochichi, the chief of the Yamacraw tribe, and Gen. James Oglethorpe, leader of the British settlers who founded the city in 1733. But then came war, yellow fever, hurricanes, and fires, not to mention pirates and curses — making the city seem, at least to the builders digging around, like one big graveyard. Savannah has turned that sordid history to its advantage: about 30 ghost tours are offered in the city, including a haunted pub crawl. Only one, though, picks you up at your hotel in an open-top hearse, **Hearse Tours** (912-695-1578; hearseghosttours.com; $15). In addition to recounting some of Savannah's most notorious murders, suicides, and deathbed tales, your joke-telling guide might share personal paranormal theories, make everyone scream in unison to spook passersby, or stop for cocktails at favorite haunts. (It's legal to take your julep for a stroll.)

SATURDAY

4 *Up-and-Coming* 10 a.m.

Venture out of the historic district to the up-and-coming area called Starland, filled with galleries and studios. Start at **Desotorow** (2427 De Soto Avenue; 912-335-8204; desotorow.org), a non-profit gallery run by current and recent art students, where exhibitions might feature adventurous drawings and collages, doll lamps, or contemporary illustration. Next, make your way up to **Maldoror's** (2418 De Soto Avenue, 912-443-5355; maldorors.com; $), a frame shop with the aura of a Victorian curio cabinet and a print collection to match. Rounding the corner, you'll come to **Back in the Day** (2403 Bull Street; 912-495-9292; backinthedaybakery.com), an old-fashioned bakery that inspires fervent loyalty among locals. Pick up one of the sandwiches, like the Madras curry chicken on ciabatta, and maybe a cupcake, to take with you for lunch.

5 *Picnic with the Dead* Noon

Few cemeteries are more stately and picnic-perfect than **Bonaventure Cemetery** (330 Bonaventure Road), with its 250-year-old live oaks draped with Spanish moss as if perpetually decorated for Halloween. The cemetery, where Conrad Aiken, Johnny Mercer, and other notable residents are buried, looks out over the intracoastal waterway and is a gathering spot for anglers as well as mourners. Find a quiet spot to ponder fate and eat your lunch.

6 *Old Streets, New Museum* 2 p.m.

The battle took years and matched two unlikely adversaries: the **Telfair Museum of Art**, the oldest art museum in the South, which wanted to expand,

ABOVE Elizabeth on 37th serves a seafood-rich menu in a palatial neoclassical-style villa built in 1900.

BELOW Hearse Tours takes visitors to the haunts of Savannah's thriving population of ghosts.

and the powerful Savannah Historic District Board of Review. The result, after intense haggling, was a light-filled building that is as trim as a yacht and has won accolades for its architect, Moshe Safdie. The addition, the **Jepson Center for the Arts** (207 West York Street; 912-790-8800; telfair.org), preserved Savannah's cherished street grid by dividing the structure into two and joining it with two glass bridges while giving the museum much-needed space. The original 19th-century museum (121 Barnard Street) is home to *The Bird Girl*, the now-famous statue that adorns the cover of *Midnight in the Garden*; she was relocated, like a federal witness, from Bonaventure Cemetery for her protection. The museum also operates tours of the nearly 200-year-old **Owens-Thomas House** (124 Abercorn Street). A combination ticket covers all three.

7 *School Fair* 5 p.m.

Shopping in Savannah is increasingly sophisticated, with recent additions like an imposing Marc by Marc Jacobs store on the rapidly gentrifying Broughton Street. But the most interesting retail is at **shopSCAD**, a boutique that sells the creations of the students, faculty, alumni, and staff of the Savannah College of Art and Design (340 Bull Street; 912-525-5180; shopscadonline.com). There is fine art —drawings, paintings, photography, and prints— as well as decorative and wearable items, including

hand-dyed ties by Jen Swearington ($48) and a pendant lamp by Christopher Moulder ($1,150).

8 *Crab Heaven* 7:30 p.m.

Forget about crab cakes, stuffed soft shells, or crabmeat au gratin. Crab is most rewarding when it is pure and unadulterated, served in a pile on newspaper with a can of beer and a blunt instrument for whacking at the shell. That, plus some boiled potatoes and corn, is what you will find at **Desposito's** (3520 Macceo Drive, Thunderbolt; 912-897-9963; $$), an unadorned shack in a onetime fishing village on the outskirts of town. This is not dining; this is working, but the sweet morsels are better than any payday.

9 *Drinking In the Scene* 9:30 p.m.

Many of Savannah's finest bars close early—often when the owners feel like it—so don't wait to start on your drink-by-drink tour. Begin at the **American Legion Post 135**, south of Forsyth Park (1108 Bull Street; 912-233-9277; alpost135.com), a surprisingly shimmery, mirrored space where the clientele is a mix of age and vocation. Proceed to the **Crystal Beer Parlor** (301 West Jones Street; 912-349-4113; crystalbeerparlor.com). On the outside, it's as

ABOVE The no-frills, low-priced Thunderbird Inn plays up its retro ambience.

anonymous as a speakeasy, which it was, but inside, its high-backed booths and colorful hanging lamps are more ice cream than booze. A full menu is available. Wind up at **Planters Tavern** (23 Abercorn Street; 912-232-4286), a noisy, low-ceilinged bar in the basement of the high-dollar Olde Pink House, a dignified restaurant in a 1771 house. With a fireplace on either end of the room, live music, and boisterous locals, it's the place to be.

SUNDAY

10 *Church's Chicken* 11 a.m.

Church and food go together in the South, and they do so especially well at the **Masada Café** (2301

West Bay Street; 912-236-9499), a buffet annex to the United House of Prayer for All People. The church has several locations in Savannah; this one is a mission of sorts, catering to the poor, but the inexpensive, revolving buffet of soul food classics like fried chicken and macaroni and cheese has gained a following among food critics and locals. Get there at 11 a.m. for the Sunday service, where the music and rhythmic hand-clapping surely share some DNA with the "ring shouts" of the Gullah-Geechee people, descendants of slaves who once lived on the nearby barrier islands.

OPPOSITE The ArtZeum inside the Jepson Center for the Arts, an addition to the Telfair Museum of Art.

THE BASICS

Fly to the Savannah/Hilton Head International Airport and take a shuttle into Savannah. The historic district is easily traversed by foot. A cab or a car may be necessary for other destinations.

Mansion on Forsyth Park
700 Drayton Street
912-238-5158
mansiononforsythpark.com
$$$
A lavish 1888 home eccentrically decorated with garish paintings and an antique hat collection.

AVIA Savannah
14 Barnard Street
912-233-2116
aviahotels.com/hotels/savannah/
$$$
New, hip boutique hotel overlooking Ellis Square.

Thunderbird Inn
611 West Oglethorpe Avenue
912-232-2661
thethunderbirdinn.com
$$
A no-frills motel refurbished with a vintage flair.

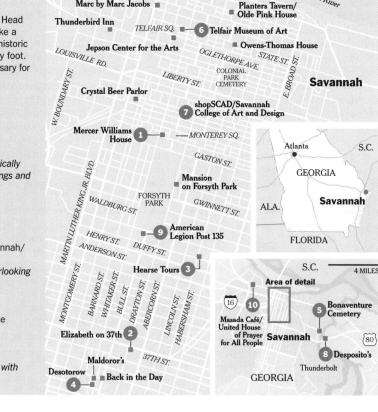

St. Simons
Island

The Golden Isles, the barrier islands of Georgia's coast, meld two worlds: the sunny beaches and lollygag pace of island life and the stately Spanish moss-draped grace of the South with antebellum graveyards and ruined plantations. St. Simons, about equidistant between Jacksonville, Fla., and Savannah, Ga., in particular is a literary haunt, home of writers' conferences and a favorite location of authors including Tina McElroy Ansa, whose popular black heroine, Lena McPherson, can see ghosts. Hidden amid the island's resorts and golf courses are remnants of the time when the only residents were Gullah-Geechee people, rice-tenders descended from slaves who speak their own blend of African languages and English. St. Simons, where oak trees turn avenues into tunnels of green, is the hub of the barrier islands, with about 13,000 residents and a bustling strip of restaurants and shops called the Village. — BY SHAILA DEWAN

FRIDAY

1 *On the Pier* 3 p.m.

Start at the **St. Simons Bait & Tackle** shop (121 Mallory Street; 912-634-1888), where you may win a greeting from the African gray parrot, Mr. Byrd (who has his own Facebook page), and rent fishing poles. Walk outside to the pier to try for anything from sheepshead to flounder, or just dangle the line in the water and daydream. A short stroll takes you to the **St. Simons Island Lighthouse**, built in 1872 after Confederates destroyed the original. It is a quaint white structure with a 360-degree observation deck overlooking St. Simons Sound and the mainland. And it gives you some exercise before you embark on a series of buttery, greasy, delicious Southern meals (912-638-4666; saintsimonslighthouse.org; arrive before 4:30 if you want to climb the tower).

2 *Crab Stew and a Beer* 5:30 p.m.

Head north on scenic Highway 17 to experience a true Georgia tradition, the seafood shack. **Hunter's Café** (there's no street address; call 912-832-5771 for

OPPOSITE The Avenue of Oaks at Sea Island resort.

RIGHT A "tree spirit" sculpture by Keith Jennings, one of several scattered around the island.

directions; $) is on a dirt road amid the marinas — or, as they are called here, fish camps — of Shellman Bluff, about a 30-minute drive toward Savannah. (The diners at the next table are likely to be fishermen just returned from a day in the salt marshes.) To the basic shack formula of bright lighting and linoleum floors, Hunter's has added a full bar and a screened porch overlooking the Broro River, but it maintains the customary disdain for any decoration not furnished by a taxidermist. Have the crab stew and fluffy oniony hushpuppies.

3 *Tree Spirits* 9 p.m.

Back on St. Simons, in the commercial district known as the Village, look for the green and yellow awning of **Murphy's Tavern** (415 Mallory Street; 912-638-8966), a favorite haunt of shrimpers, summer residents, and townies. Order a beer, pick someone out and suggest a game of pool. Outside, look for the face of a "tree spirit" carved into a huge old oak tree. A handful of these spirits, sculptures by Keith Jennings, are on public sites scattered around St. Simons; more are hidden away on private property.

SATURDAY

4 *The Breakfast Rush* 9 a.m.

Sit on the front patio and feast on the seafood omelet or the butter pecan French toast at the **4th**

of May Café (321 Mallory Street; 912-638-5444; 4thofmay.net; $), a popular Village restaurant named after the common birthday of the three original owners (two were twins). You're early, so you should beat the rush of retirees, young couples, families, tourists, and regulars who descend like gulls for breakfast.

5 *The Little Island* 10:30 a.m.

If you doze off when you hear the phrase "bird-watcher's paradise," just forget about the bird part and catch the boat to **Little St. Simons Island**, a private retreat where you can spend the day lying on the beach and touring the near-pristine live oak and magnolia forest. Two of the resort's main buildings are an old hunting lodge and a stunning cottage made of tabby, a stuccolike material of lime and oyster shells. Family owned, the resort is also family style, which means help yourself to towels, sunscreen, bug spray, and the beer set out in coolers on the porch. Most of the island has been left virtually untouched, and it is possible in one day to observe river otter, dolphins, the endangered greenfly orchid, and bald eagles, as well as roseate spoonbills and a host of other birds. The beach is littered with sand dollars and conch. A day trip is $75 a person and includes lunch, transportation to and from the island, a naturalist-guided tour, and time at the beach. You'll leave from the Hampton River Club Marina (1000 Hampton Point Drive on St. Simons) at 10:30 and will be back by 4:30. Reservations are required (the Lodge on Little St. Simons Island; 912-638-7472; littlessi.com).

6 *Alligator Hazard* 5:30 p.m.

Back on the big island, there's still time for nine holes of golf ($54) at the **King and Prince Golf Course**

ABOVE Christ Church, built by a lumber magnate mourning the death of his wife on their honeymoon.

RIGHT The King and Prince Golf Course, where you might see an alligator eyeing the golfers.

(100 Tabbystone; 912-634-0255; hamptonclub.com), a course that makes full use of the starkly beautiful marsh landscape. Ask to play 10 through 18; four of these holes are on little marsh islands connected by bridges. You'll putt surrounded by a sea of golden grasses that even non-golfers will appreciate. One hole is near an island with a resident alligator.

7 *Upscale Seafood* 8 p.m.

Settle in for drinks and a leisurely dinner at one of the fancy restaurants like **Halyards**, featuring Southern seafood dishes (55 Cinema Lane; 912-638-9100; halyardsrestaurant.com; $$-$$$), or the more traditional **Georgia Sea Grill** (310 Mallory Street; 912-638-1197; $$-$$$).

SUNDAY

8 *Church with a Past* 10 a.m.

It has history, it has literary significance, it has a tragic love story. But the thing to notice at Christ Church, Frederica, built in 1884 by a lumber magnate mourning the death of his wife on their honeymoon, is the thick, lambent lawn, one of the great unnoticed triumphs of Southern horticulture. **Christ Church, Frederica** (6329 Frederica Road; 912-638-8683) was a setting in a novel by Eugenia Price, who is buried in the graveyard there. The oldest grave dates to 1803. Across the street is a wooded garden dedicated

to Charles and John Wesley, who preached on St. Simons in the 1730s as Anglicans; they later returned to England and founded the Methodist Church.

9 *Bicycle-Friendly* 11:30 a.m.

The exclusive **Lodge at Sea Island** (100 Retreat Avenue; 912-638-3611; seaisland.com) is off limits to all but guests and members. But if you go by bike you may be able to sneak a peek of its grounds and the ruins of Retreat Plantation's hospital, where slaves were treated. You'll also experience the island's bicycle-friendly avenues, lined with tremendous 150-year-old oaks. Rent a bike for $15 to $20 a day at **Ocean Motion** (1300 Ocean Boulevard; 912-638-5225) or **Wheel Fun Rentals** (532 Ocean Boulevard; 912-634-0606),

head south following the road around the tip of the island, and make a left on Frederica Road to reach the Avenue of Oaks, which leads to the guard house of the Lodge before it loops back to Frederica Road. You can ask to see the ruins just inside the grounds. If you're ambitious, venture onto the Torras Causeway, which leads to the mainland and has a bike path.

ABOVE Rent a fishing pole and drop in a line.

THE BASICS

Fly into Savannah/Hilton Head International Airport or Jacksonville International Airport. Rent a car for the 90-minute drive from either airport, and then use it to stay mobile.

King and Prince Beach & Golf Resort
201 Arnold Road
912-638-3631
kingandprince.com
$$$-$$$$
A sprawling 75-year-old full-service resort with guest rooms, villas, and cabanas.

The Lodge at Sea Island Resorts
100 Retreat Avenue
866-879-6238
seaisland.com
$$$$
Close to golf courses; 24-hour butler service.

Ocean Inn & Suites
599 Beachview Drive
912-634-2122
oceaninnsuites.com
$-$$
Within walking distance of the Village and the lighthouse.

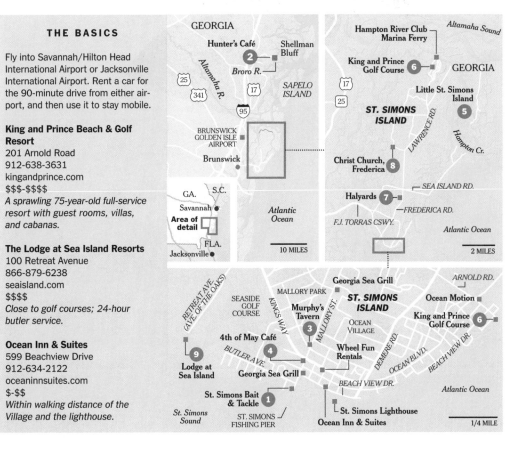

Orlando

People who live in the Orlando area will tell you that there is life here beyond the theme parks, gator farms, and citrus groves. You can't go far without stumbling upon a picturesque lake, and the area abounds with small regional museums like the Zora Neale Hurston National Museum of Fine Arts in nearby Eatonville. Downtown, the new Amway Center, home of the Orlando Magic, has given a boost to the nightlife district on Church Street. And Orlando's many neighborhoods are home to lounge acts, bars, vintage fast-food joints, and brick-paved streets. — BY SHAILA DEWAN

FRIDAY

1 *Plunge In* 2 p.m.

Wakeboarding is to water skiing what snowboarding is to downhill skiing—in other words, the extreme version of the sport—and Orlando likes to call itself the "wakeboarding capital of the world." At the **Orlando Watersports Complex** (8615 Florida Rock Road; 407-251-3100; orlandowatersports.com), a beginner's cable tow, anchored to poles in the lake, pulls you and your wakeboard around at 17 miles per hour. The patient instructor will give you pointers, and you can watch some of the sport's best-known hot-doggers navigate the ramps and slides.

2 *High Design* 5 p.m.

Just a few miles from downtown Orlando, Winter Park—considered part of the greater Orlando area—is famous for the brick-paved streets of chichi chocolatiers and boutiques along Park Avenue. But across the railroad tracks near Hannibal Square, a coda has popped up with a bent toward high design. Amid the new shops and restaurants, you can find **Rifle Paper Co.** (558 West New England Avenue, Suite 150; 407-622-7679; riflepaperco.com), the fashionable Orlando-based stationer, and the studio and storefront where **Makr Carry Goods** churns out its minimalist leather bags and iPod cases (444 West New England Avenue, Suite 102; 407-284-0192; makr.com).

OPPOSITE Wakeboarding on the advanced cable tow at the Orlando Watersports Complex.

RIGHT The strip-mall location may be uninspiring, but dinner at the Ravenous Pig in Winter Park is worth the trip.

For a taste of local history, visit the **Hannibal Square Heritage Center** (642 West New England Avenue; 407-539-2680; hannibalsquareheritagecenter.org), where a collection of photographs and oral histories document the area's early role as a Reconstruction-era community for freed slaves.

3 *Dress Up, Dress Down* 7 p.m.

From the outside, the **Ravenous Pig** (1234 North Orange Avenue, Winter Park; 407-628-2333; theravenouspig.com; $$$) looks like your average strip-mall restaurant. But with attention to detail like house-made sour mix at the bar and much-in-demand cheese biscuits, James and Julie Petrakis have made their gastropub one of Orlando's most popular gathering spots. The menu, like the restaurant, is dress-up/dress-down, with bar fare like mussels and fries dusted with fennel pollen or more dignified entrees like dry-aged strip steak with wild mushroom bread pudding. Reserve a table or hover in the bar.

4 *Lounge Act* 10 p.m.

If the **Red Fox Lounge** (110 South Orlando Avenue, Winter Park; 407-647-1166) were an amusement park, it might be called ToupeeWorld. This stuck-in-amber hotel bar in a Best Western hotel appeals to a broad cross-section of Orlando, from retirees to young professionals to a drinking club whose members wear identical captain's hats. The main draw is the consummate lounge act. Mark Wayne and Lorna Lambey deliver silky, singalong versions of "Sweet Caroline," "Hava Nagila," and other golden oldies.

SATURDAY

5 *Tiffany Extravaganza* 10 a.m.

Louis Comfort Tiffany's masterpiece was Laurelton Hall, his estate on Long Island, which featured a wisteria blossom window over 30 feet long and a terrace whose columns were crowned in glass daffodils. When the house burned in 1957, Jeanette and Hugh McKean, from Winter Park, rescued those pieces and many more, adding them to what would become the most comprehensive collection of Tiffany glass, jewelry, and ceramics in the world. The collection, including a chapel with a stunning peacock mosaic that was made for the Chicago World's Fair in 1893, is housed in the **Morse Museum of American Art** (445 North Park Avenue, Winter Park; 407-645-5311; morsemuseum.org), where a new wing allows the largest Laurelton Hall pieces, including the daffodil terrace, to be on permanent display.

6 *A Fast-Food Original* Noon

Devotees of American fast food in all its glory will not want to miss the roast beef sandwiches and cherry milkshakes at **Beefy King**, a lunchtime standby for more than four decades (424 North Bumby Avenue; 407-894-2241; beefyking.com; $). Perch on the old-fashioned swivel chairs and admire the vintage logo of a snorting steer, also available on hot pink T-shirts.

7 *Pontoon Tour* 3 p.m.

Orlando is not quite an American Venice, but it does have about 100 lakes, many connected by narrow canals. Despite the alligators, the lakes are prime real estate, and at **Lake Osceola**, you can board a pontoon boat and take an hourlong cruise (**Scenic Boat Tour;** 312 East Morse Boulevard; 407-644-4056; scenicboattours.com) that will provide glimpses of Spanish colonial-style mansions, azalea gardens, stately Rollins College, and moss-laden cypresses. The ride is billed as Florida's longest continuously running tourist attraction, though you are likely to find plenty of locals aboard. The guide will entertain you with celebrity anecdotes, a smattering of history, and a reasonably small number of cheesy jokes. Tours leave on the hour.

8 *Cultural Fusion* 6 p.m.

The city of theme parks does have a studious side, as evidenced in a blossoming neighborhood called College Park, where the streets have names like Harvard and Vassar and where Jack Kerouac wrote *Dharma Bums*. The main commercial drag, Edgewater Drive, is chockablock with local favorites like **K Restaurant** (1710 Edgewater Drive; 407-872-2332; kwinebar.com; $$), where the servers'

ABOVE The Morse Museum of American Art.

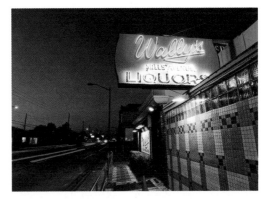

habit of asking for and using your name makes you feel like a regular. With an appetizer of crispy pig's ear on a salad with peanuts and cilantro, the chef gives a nod to Vietnamese flavors that abound in Orlando. At **Infusion Tea** (1600 Edgewater Drive; 407-999-5255; infusionorlando.com; $), choose from dozens of loose teas like Organic Monkey-Picked Oolong to go along with chocolate-coated Cheerios or a cupcake. Or you can choose among the scarves, vintage aprons, and jewelry at the attached artists' collective.

9 *Dive-Bar Hopping* 10 p.m.

Stiff drinks and dive bars are an Orlando staple; much of the night life is centered in the ViMi district, for Virginia Drive and Mills Avenue. Arguably the king of dives is **Wally's Mills Avenue Liquors** (1001 North Mills Avenue; 407-896-6975), with a U-shaped bar and tobacco-stained wallpaper with a motif of naked women. Across the street is the concrete-floored **LMGA**, or Lou's Music, Gaming, and Alcohol (1016 North Mills Avenue; 407-898-0009; myspace.com/unclelousorlando), where the owner,

known as Uncle Lou, wears headphones to block out noise of band concerts. Farther down, **Will's Pub** (1042 North Mills Avenue; 407-898-5070; myspace.com/willspub) has pool tables and indie bands.

SUNDAY

10 *Sweet Potato Hash* 11 a.m.

You never know what will turn up on the improvised brunch menu—a slip of notebook paper with a ballpoint scrawl—at **Stardust Video and Coffee** (1842 East Winter Park Road, 407-623-3393; $), a hub for

ABOVE Wally's, a stop on the dive-bar circuit.

BELOW A Winter Park canal, part of the Orlando area's abundant supply of lakes and connecting waterways.

Orlando's artistic class. Zucchini pancakes, maybe, or vegan sweet potato hash with eggs and (real) bacon. The Web site advertises "bathroom yoga" and "parking lot bingo," but you're more likely to find art installations, an old-fashioned photo booth, and a slew of obscure videos and DVDs for rent on the shelves at the far end of this sunny, airy space. There is a full bar for the performances, screenings, and lectures that unfold here in the later hours.

11 *Fool's Gold, Real Finds* 2 p.m.

Flea markets can offer too many tube socks and T-shirts, while antiques markets can be entirely too stuffy. **Renningers Twin Markets** in Mount Dora (20651 Highway 441; renningers.com), about a 30-minute drive from downtown, puts the thrill back in the hunt. Just past the main entrance, you can turn right and head to a vast antiques barn crammed with treasures like meticulously constructed wooden model ships and 19th-century quilts. Or you can turn left for the flea and farmers' market, where home-grown orchids and leather motorcycle chaps compete for attention. Behind that, there is a field where curio dealers set up tables with all manner of bona fide junk, fool's gold, and the occasional real finds that make it clear why so many thrift aficionados make road trips to Florida.

OPPOSITE The Morse Museum of American Art displays an extensive collection of works by Louis Comfort Tiffany.

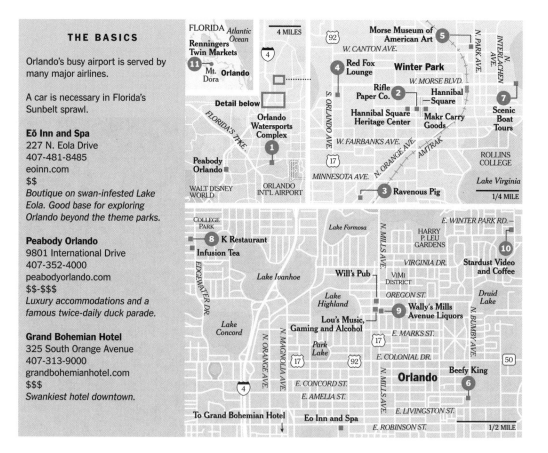

THE BASICS

Orlando's busy airport is served by many major airlines.

A car is necessary in Florida's Sunbelt sprawl.

Eō Inn and Spa
227 N. Eola Drive
407-481-8485
eoinn.com
$$
Boutique on swan-infested Lake Eola. Good base for exploring Orlando beyond the theme parks.

Peabody Orlando
9801 International Drive
407-352-4000
peabodyorlando.com
$$-$$$
Luxury accommodations and a famous twice-daily duck parade.

Grand Bohemian Hotel
325 South Orange Avenue
407-313-9000
grandbohemianhotel.com
$$$
Swankiest hotel downtown.

Cape Canaveral

The glory days of the space program, when regular flights to the moon left from Cape Canaveral, are far in the past, but NASA still has a presence, the local area code is still 321, and the Kennedy Space Center remains the conservator of proud national memories. In other ways, this part of Florida is still coming into its own. Cocoa Beach, just south on the long stretch of barrier sand and islands off the state's central Atlantic coast, has been thoroughly discovered, though it still feels almost unspoiled in comparison to the condo-towered shores of South Florida. Canaveral has emerged as a busy cruise port. And there's more to see, from citrus groves and wild protected seashores to one of the country's best surf shops. Feeling hungry? You can dine on fine French cuisine or fresh Florida seafood — or just head to a local souvenir shop for some freeze-dried ice cream, an astronaut favorite.
— BY CHARLES PASSY

FRIDAY

1 *Ocean Outreach* 6 p.m.

The lovably scruffy side of an older Florida reveals itself at the **Cocoa Beach Pier** (401 Meade Avenue, Cocoa Beach; cocoabeachpier.com), a 44-year-old hangout that stretches some 800 feet into the Atlantic Ocean. You come here to drink, dine, or fish — the pier is dotted with stores, bars, and restaurants, both indoors and outdoors — or just take in the expansive view. The pier scene really hops during the Friday-night Boardwalk Bash, when bands perform. Enjoy a cold one and some bar fare (wings, burgers, fish and chips) at **Marlins Good Times Bar & Grill** while listening to the music.

2 *Hang 10, 24/7* 8 p.m.

Who doesn't feel the need to go surfboard shopping on a Friday night? O.K., so maybe you're not ready to plunk down $1,000 to ride the waves in style, but the selections at the justly famous flagship **Ron Jon Surf Shop** (4151 North Atlantic Avenue, Cocoa Beach; 321-799-8888; ronjonsurfshop.com)

OPPOSITE The Rocket Garden at the Kennedy Space Center.

RIGHT Partying comes with a view at the Cocoa Beach Pier, which juts 800 feet out into the Atlantic.

go beyond boards and surfing gear. The two-story, 52,000-square-foot store, which is open 24 hours a day — and claims to be visited by more than two million people annually — also sells beachwear, shot glasses, Polynesian kitsch, and other "why did I buy that?" items. A spirit of endless hooky pervades, as evidenced by the T-shirt for sale that says, "I was on summer vacation for 20 years."

SATURDAY

3 *Breakfast Cubano* 8 a.m.

While Cuban food is most associated with the Miami area, the Canaveral area can lay claim to one of the state's best spots — **Roberto's Little Havana Restaurant** (26 North Orlando Avenue, Cocoa Beach; 321-784-1868; robertoslittlehavana.com; $). It's a downtown Cocoa Beach favorite serving all the Cuban classics, from palomilla steak to fried yuca to flan. But at breakfast time, it's the place to be for an egg-bacon-cheese sandwich, served on soft Cuban bread. Good Cuban coffee, too.

4 *Citrus Stop* 9:30 a.m.

You're a few miles from the Indian River fruit area that is one of Florida's legendary spots for citrus groves. So you'll have to stop for some liquid sunshine. **Policicchio Groves** (5780 North Courtenay Parkway (Route 3); Merritt Island; 321-452-4866;

juicycitrus.com), a family enterprise nearly nine decades old, has an assortment of oranges and grapefruits; the varieties change each month during the winter and the spring-to-early-summer growing seasons. Everything is freshly picked; the groves are across the road. The store will help you pack and ship the bounty.

5 *A Space Odyssey* 10:30 a.m.

Go north on Route 3 and left on NASA Parkway (Route 405) for the **Kennedy Space Center Visitor Complex** (321-449-4444; kennedyspacecenter.com). The complex may vaguely resemble one of Florida's theme parks at first, and the ticket prices suggest something of the kind. But very soon it becomes much more inspiring. Start with a walk through the Rocket Garden, an open-air space that features awe-inspiring Redstone, Atlas, and Titan rockets that date from the days of the Mercury and Gemini missions; you can also squeeze into replicas of the capsules the astronauts used. But that's the appetizer to the space center's main course — a roughly three-hour bus tour that gives you a sense of how big the center truly is (some 140,000 acres, including the surrounding wildlife refuge). Along the way, you'll pass the Vehicle Assembly Building — a structure so cavernous that clouds are said to have formed inside it. The tour's most jaw-dropping stop is the Apollo/Saturn V Center, a huge hangar that contains an actual Saturn V rocket. Take time to look at the individual exhibits about the Apollo program, all presented with extraordinary detail.

6 *Close Encounter* 2:45 p.m.

Now that you've gotten yourself acquainted (or reacquainted) with the space program, it's time to meet a real astronaut. The center's Astronaut Encounter affords an opportunity to do just that. Veterans of the space program, mostly from the shuttle era, give daily 30-minute presentations about their experiences and field questions from the audience. (There are at least three presentations

daily, with one generally at mid-afternoon.) Want a little more face time? For an extra fee, you can sign up for lunch with an astronaut. Among those who have participated in both the encounter and lunch programs are the Apollo 15 astronaut Al Worden and the six-time shuttle veteran Story Musgrave.

7 *Astronaut Memorial* 3:30 p.m.

About two dozen astronauts have died in their attempts to slip "the surly bonds of earth," as the World War II pilot John Gillespie Magee Jr. put it in a poem quoted by President Reagan after the 1986 Challenger disaster. Those men and women are remembered at the center's simple, stark Space Mirror Memorial — a black granite surface in which the names are inscribed. When the light is at the right angle, the names seem to float in space.

8 *Au Côte d'Espace* 7 p.m.

The Cape Canaveral area may not be a citadel of fine dining, but **Café Margaux** (220 Brevard Avenue, Cocoa; 321-639-8343; cafemargaux.com; $$$) is an exception to the rule. This quaint restaurant, set in the tree-lined Cocoa Village district, is proudly French, with a few nods elsewhere. The wine list places equal emphasis on New and Old World vintages.

SUNDAY

9 *Natural Habitat* 10 a.m.

It takes a lot of surrounding land to keep the Kennedy Space Center's launch sites properly isolated. Much of that acreage is encompassed

within the buffer zone that is the **Merritt Island National Wildlife Refuge** (321-861-0667; fws.gov/merrittisland), a huge, mostly untouched tract that is home to migratory birds and bald eagles. Begin your journey by picking up a map at one of the kiosks near the entrances to the refuge (the small visitor's center may be closed if you're in the wrong season), and then head to the gloriously remote beaches, which are part of the separately managed **Canaveral National Seashore** (321-267-1110; nps.gov/cana). Conclude with a visit to the refuge's Black Point Wildlife Drive — a seven-mile loop that allows you to get close to wildlife, including alligators and egrets, without leaving your car.

10 *In the Realm of the Shrimp* 1 p.m.
The family-owned **Dixie Crossroads Seafood Restaurant** (1475 Garden Street, Titusville; 321-268-5000; dixiecrossroads.com; $$-$$$) is mostly

about shrimp. It has its own fleet of about 10 full-time commercial shrimpers, which provide the restaurant with its lobsterlike rock shrimp and more firmly textured Royal Red shrimp, among other Florida varieties. (Once you try these, you'll find it hard to go back to garden-variety frozen shrimp.) The shrimp can be had broiled, fried, or steamed. But before you dig in, you'll get to enjoy the corn fritter starters included with every meal. The bustling setting is also a hoot — part Old Florida (wildlife murals and a fish pond), part pure kitsch. You can pose outside with Mr. and Mrs. Rock — cartoonish statues of a rock shrimp family.

OPPOSITE ABOVE Sunrise surfing at the pier.

OPPOSITE BELOW Oranges for the buying at Policicchio Groves. Florida's famous Indian River citrus-growing region is just inland from Cape Canaveral.

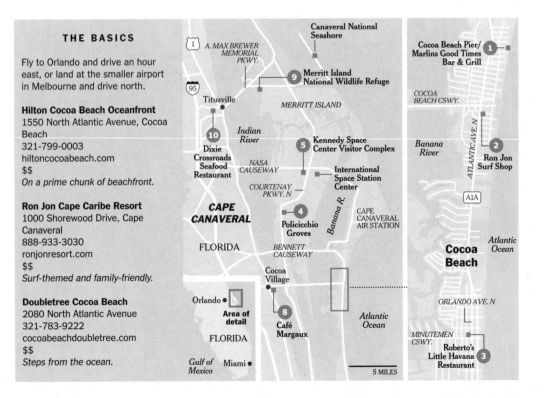

THE BASICS

Fly to Orlando and drive an hour east, or land at the smaller airport in Melbourne and drive north.

Hilton Cocoa Beach Oceanfront
1550 North Atlantic Avenue, Cocoa Beach
321-799-0003
hiltoncocoabeach.com
$$
On a prime chunk of beachfront.

Ron Jon Cape Caribe Resort
1000 Shorewood Drive, Cape Canaveral
888-933-3030
ronjonresort.com
$$
Surf-themed and family-friendly.

Doubletree Cocoa Beach
2080 North Atlantic Avenue
321-783-9222
cocoabeachdoubletree.com
$$
Steps from the ocean.

5 MILES

Palm Beach

The tiny island of Palm Beach, on Florida's southeast coast, boasts some of the country's dreamiest estates, where the staff lives better than many Americans, cashmere sweaters in trademark pastel greens and pinks go for $800, and Rolls-Royces show up at the supermarket with regularity. Some Palm Beachers had to tighten their Gucci belts in the wake of the Bernard Madoff scandal; he selected many of his victims at the local golf club. But judging by the perfectly clipped hedges that envelop the manicured mansions, most residents may be doing with less, but not much less, in a town where more is never quite enough.

— BY GERALDINE FABRIKANT

FRIDAY

1 *The Big Gape* 4 p.m.

Big money means big house, so rent a nice convertible and stare. For envy-inducing views of these winter palaces, drive south along **South Ocean Boulevard** for about six miles starting at Barton Avenue. Even those obsessed with privacy relish their ocean views (why pay millions for beachfront if you can't enjoy it?), which means the gates and hedges along these mansions are slightly lower than elsewhere in town. You can catch a glimpse of the Mar-a-Lago Club, Donald Trump's former residence and now a private club he owns.

2 *Grande Dame* 6:30 p.m.

For a sunset cocktail, glide into the **Breakers Hotel** (1 South County Road; 561-655-6611; thebreakers.com), originally built in 1896. So central is its location that the hotel has been rebuilt twice after fires destroyed it. The Seafood Bar has delightful views of the sea. If you prefer upholstered opulence, head for the Tapestry Bar with its two Flemish tapestries and a grand bar built from a mantel from Caxton Hall in London.

3 *Diner's Club* 8:30 p.m.

Palm Beach dining runs from supremely pretentious to casually simple. Many restaurants survive over decades, and because Palm Beach is a small town, where the same cast shows up frequently, they have the feel of private clubs. The **Palm Beach Grill** (340 Royal Poinciana Way; 561-835-1077; palmbeachgrill.com; $$$) is a darkly wooded, dimly

lighted social fixture that is a favorite of the author James Patterson and almost everyone else. If the mobbed dining room is for the island's old guard, the bar seems to attract newcomers: snowbirds deciding whether to move South, city types longing for a slower, more glamorous life, and locals who want to have fun. Don't miss American classics like spare ribs and ice cream sundaes. Book before you fly.

SATURDAY

4 *Empty Beaches* 8 a.m.

Park on **South Ocean Boulevard** and take a long, languorous walk on the beach. The beaches here are flat, wide, clean, and wonderful in the early morning when there are not many people around.

5 *Early Snowbirds* 9 a.m.

This may be a party town, but it wakes up early. A clutch of restaurants along Royal Poinciana Way are busy by 8:30 a.m., with diners sitting outside and savoring the sunshine and breakfast. **Testa's**

OPPOSITE The lobby at the Breakers, the iconic Palm Beach hotel where the wealthy have long come to be pampered.

BELOW For drive-by glimpses of the waterfront mansions, head out along South Ocean Boulevard.

Palm Beach Restaurant (221 Royal Poinciana Way; 561-832-0992; testasrestaurants.com; $$), a sprawling, relaxed space, serves blueberry, pecan, and bran pancakes. Around the corner is **Green's Pharmacy** (151 North County Road; 561-832-4443; $$), which offers breakfast at an old-fashioned lunch counter. Afterward, pick up candy buttons and other long-forgotten stuff.

6 *History Class* 10:30 a.m.

For an authentic sense of Palm Beach in its early days, drop by the **Flagler Museum** (1 Whitehall Way; 561-655-2833; flaglermuseum.us). It was once the home of Henry Morrison Flagler, one of the founders of Standard Oil and the man who brought the railroad to southern Florida. He spent millions in 1902 to build the 55-room house that became a hotel and finally a museum.

7 *Retail Strut* Noon

On Worth Avenue, where every brand that you've seen in *Vogue* has a storefront, the real fun is the crowd: women in green cashmere sweaters walking dogs in matching outfits; elderly gents with bow ties and blazers. But the true gems — Cartier aside — are the smaller, lesser-known stores that have survived by wit and originality. **Maryanna Suzanna** (313 Worth Avenue; 561-833-0204) carries colorful jewelry by Monies and the Italian designer Angela Caputi — some earrings are under $50. Across the street, **Sherry Frankel's Melangerie** (256 Worth Avenue; 561-655-1996) will custom-embroider anything and sells amusing plastic watches for $68. And nearby is **Il Sandalo** (240 Worth Avenue; 561-805-8674; ilsandalo.com), where the shoemaker

ABOVE The Flagler Museum, once the lavish home of Henry Clay Flagler, a founder of Standard Oil. One of the items on display is his private railway car.

RIGHT The Blue Martini in West Palm Beach, the humbler sister town across the Intracoastal Waterway.

Hernan Garcia makes custom sandals starting at around $200. For lunch, head to **Ta-boo** (221 Worth Avenue; 561-835-3500; taboorestaurant.com; $$$), with its British colonial décor, where women swathed in white linen and wearing enormous straw hats pick carefully at the chopped chef's salad.

8 *Gilt Trip* 3:30 p.m.

It's a challenge to fill those sprawling estates with furniture, but there are armies of antiques merchants poised to try. Antiques enthusiasts can start at the elegant French dealer **Cedric Dupont** (820 South Dixie Highway; 561-835-1319; cedricdupontantiques.com) and go all the way south to Southern Boulevard to **The Elephant's Foot** (3800 South Dixie Highway; 561-832-0170; theelephantsfootantiques.com), which has a range of English, French, and Oriental antiques at varying prices. Or for a resale find, try **Circa Who** (531 Northwood Road; 561-655-5224; circawho.com), with faux bamboo, and Old Florida furniture.

9 *Mediterranean Flavor* 8 p.m.

For a casual dinner in the heart of town, head to **Cucina Dell'Arte** (257 Royal Poinciana Way; 561-655-0770; cucinadellarte.com; $$$), which is popular with a younger crowd and is open until 3 a.m. It is decorated in the earth tones and mustards and peaches typical of the Mediterranean and seems

to be busy all day with families, couples, and groups of friends. You can eat outdoors and watch the crowds go by.

10 *Party Time* 10:30 p.m.

There are plenty of multi-carat jewels in Palm Beach, but they are generally worn at private parties. The night life for visitors is casual. Stop in for a drink at the very pretty **Brazilian Court Hotel** (301 Australian Avenue; 561-655-7740; thebraziliancourt.com). You might try a Bikini Martini, with Sagatiba cachaça and passion fruit purée. On Saturdays a small band or D.J. plays in the lobby until 1 a.m., attracting a preppy crowd. Or head across the bridge to **Blue Martini** (CityPlace, 550 South Rosemary Avenue, West Palm Beach; 561-835-8601; bluemartinilounge.com) in a trendy shopping mall, where you can sip a martini and hear the music pour out of B. B. King's Blues Club next door.

SUNDAY

11 *Hit the Trail* 10 a.m.

A flat and easy bike trail hugs the Intracoastal Waterway, which skirts the west side of Palm Beach, and offers fantastic views of the Marina in West Palm Beach. Rent a bike at **Palm Beach Bicycle Trail Shop** (223 Sunrise Avenue; 561-659-4583; palmbeachbicycle.com), which has multispeed bikes. If biking is not your thing, you can jog the route.

ABOVE Palm Beach feels exclusive, but the beach is public. Walk it in the early morning, when few people are out.

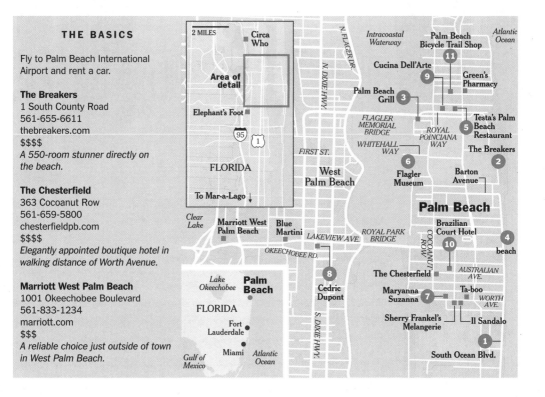

THE BASICS

Fly to Palm Beach International Airport and rent a car.

The Breakers
1 South County Road
561-655-6611
thebreakers.com
$$$$
A 550-room stunner directly on the beach.

The Chesterfield
363 Cocoanut Row
561-659-5800
chesterfieldpb.com
$$$$
Elegantly appointed boutique hotel in walking distance of Worth Avenue.

Marriott West Palm Beach
1001 Okeechobee Boulevard
561-833-1234
marriott.com
$$$
A reliable choice just outside of town in West Palm Beach.

Fort Lauderdale

Fort Lauderdale continues to mature beyond its spring-break days, with posh resorts now rising along the beach. Meanwhile, Las Olas Boulevard, the lively commercial strip that links the beach to downtown, has welcomed an array of new boutiques and restaurants. Sure, a smattering of raucous bars still dot the beach, and the rowdy clubgoers of Himmarshee Village can be three deep in the middle of the week. But at the end of a sunny, water-logged day, this Florida resort town offers a sophisticated evening that doesn't involve neon bikinis and syrupy daiquiris. — BY GERALDINE FABRIKANT

FRIDAY

1 *Seaside Dusk* 5 p.m.

There are a slew of beachfront spots where you can have a drink, watch the clouds roll over the ocean, soak up the sea air, and catch the parade of sun-soaked tourists and residents going home in suits and ties. Two of the more welcoming are **Margarita Cantina Crab and Seafood House** (201 Fort Lauderdale Beach Boulevard; 954-463-7209), where you can sip a chardonnay and listen to the steel band, and the quieter **H2O Café** (101 South Fort Lauderdale Beach Boulevard; 954-414-1024; h2ocafe.net) next door.

2 *Waterfront Wahoo* 7 p.m.

Fort Lauderdale's dining scene is alive and well inland as well as on the water. The **Bimini Boatyard Bar and Grill** (1555 Southeast 17th Street; 954-525-7400; biminiboatyard.com; $$) evokes a New England-style boathouse with its crisp blue and white décor, enormous cathedral ceiling, gleaming oak floors, and portal-style windows. An outdoor bar facing a marina brings in a nautical mix of young and old who dine on fresh seafood like wood-grilled wahoo and yellowtail snapper.

3 *Nice and Cool* 9 p.m.

For a cool nightcap, slide over to **Blue Jean Blues** (3320 Northeast 33rd Street; 954-306-6330;

OPPOSITE Sunrise at Anglin's Pier.

RIGHT The International Swimming Hall of Fame. Among the curious facts to learn inside: Leonardo da Vinci and Benjamin Franklin both experimented with swim fins.

bluejeanblues.net), where you can sit at the bar and listen to live jazz and blues bands. The club has a tiny stage and a dance floor, and the music can go from jazz to Caribbean depending on the evening.

SATURDAY

4 *Dawn Patrol* 8 a.m.

Take an early morning stroll along the wide, white beach. It is open to joggers, walkers, and swimmers and is surprisingly clean. For a leafier, more secluded adventure that is a favorite with resident runners and walkers, try the two-mile loop through the woods in the **Hugh Taylor Birch State Park** (954-468-2791; floridastateparks.org/hughtaylorbirch). Its entrance is only steps from the beach at the intersection of A1A and Sunrise Highway. If you're not a jogger, take a drive through anyway.

5 *Sunny Nosh* 10 a.m.

Finish off the jog at the beachside **Ritz-Carlton** (1 North Fort Lauderdale Beach Boulevard; 954-465-2300; ritzcarlton.com/fortlauderdale). The Ritz-Carlton Hotel Company bought the former St. Regis and put its own stamp on the property. For a relaxed breakfast (served until 11 a.m.), either indoors or out, go to **Via Luna** ($$$), the hotel's restaurant, where you can choose your fare from a buffet with omelets, smoked salmon, cereals, and fruit.

6 *Eccentric Estate* 1 p.m.

Bonnet House (900 North Birch Road; 954-563-5393; bonnethouse.org) was the vacation

home of the artists and art patrons Frederic Bartlett and his wife, Evelyn, whose first husband was the grandson and namesake of the founder of Eli Lilly and Company. They created an eccentric, brightly painted retreat, now a museum — more Caribbean mansion than Florida estate — near a swamp where alligators thrived. Window bars protected the house from the panthers that once roamed the estate and the monkeys that still live there.

7 *Cruising the Pier* 3:30 p.m.

If you want to go a bit off the beaten track, drive up Route A1A to Commercial Boulevard and hang out on **Anglin's Pier**. There is a little shopping area for swim gear, and you can rent a fishing pole. Or just sit and have a coffee.

8 *Crabs or Pizza* 7 p.m.

One of the trendier new restaurants is **Truluck's**, at the Galleria Mall (2584A East Sunrise Boulevard; 954-396-5656; trulucks.com; $$$$). An elegant room with dark woods and red leather upholstery, it adds a bit of glamour to the popular mall and has a busy bar where a piano player entertains all evening. It has a surf-and-turf menu but is perhaps best known for stone crabs. For lighter fare, try **D'Angelo** (4215 North Federal Highway, Oakland Park; 954-561-7300; pizzadangelo.com; $), a modern Tuscan-style restaurant. It attracts a fashion-aware young crowd with its meatball tapas and Napoletana pizzas.

9 *Mall Party* 9 p.m.

It may not be spring break, but you would never know, looking at the huge crowds at the **Blue Martini**, at the Galleria Mall (2432 East Sunrise Boulevard; 954-653-2583; bluemartinilounge.com). But the patrons are decidedly more upscale. By 8 p.m. when the band is playing, the bar is packed with young professionals and snow birds, schmoozing and dancing. A newer place is **SoLita Las Olas** (1032 East Las Olas; 954-357-2616; solitalasolas.com), which has a lively bar. Fort Lauderdale also has a booming gay

night-life scene; one spot to try is the ever-popular **Georgie's Alibi** (2266 Wilton Drive; 954-565-2526; georgiesalibi.com).

SUNDAY

10 *Southern Comfort* 11 a.m.

The **Pelican Grand Beach Resort** (2000 North Ocean Boulevard; 954-568-9431; pelicanbeach.com) offers a Sunday brunch with eggs Benedict, rice pilaf, bloody marys, and mimosas. The plantation-style restaurant overlooks the beach, with a big veranda with white wicker tables and rocking chairs that catch the sea breezes.

11 *Super Swimmers* 12:30 p.m.

Water enthusiasts should stop in at the **International Swimming Hall of Fame** (One Hall of Fame Drive; 954-462-6536; ishof.org). Did you know that both Leonardo da Vinci and Benjamin Franklin experimented with swim fins? Or that Polynesian

ABOVE The Bonnet House museum was the vacation home of the artists Frederic and Evelyn Bartlett in the days when panthers roamed the nearby swamps.

BELOW Morning exercise on the beach, with plenty of room for joggers, earlybird swimmers, and martial artists.

swimmers used palm leaves tied to their feet? Those and other nuggets of swimming trivia are lovingly conveyed at this sleek white building on the Intracoastal Waterway.

12 *Las Olas Stroll* 2 p.m.

In an era when shopping in new cities can remind you of every mall back home, Fort Lauderdale has kept its streak of independence: nothing fancy but fun. East Las Olas Boulevard has a rash of one-off stores. **Kumbaya** (No. 1012; 954-768-9004) carries colorful T-shirts and straw bags. **Seldom Seen Gallery** (No. 817; 954-527-7878; seldomseengallery.com) has a riot of wall clocks as well as brightly painted walking sticks. If you want

to take edible gifts home or you can't resist them yourself, drop in at **Kilwin's**, an ice cream, chocolate, and fudge shop (No. 809; 954-523-8338; kilwins. com). Its motto is "Life is uncertain. Eat dessert first." Ponder that over a bag of caramel corn as you explore the rest of the shops.

ABOVE Truluck's, a glamorous dinner spot known for seafood, especially its stone crab.

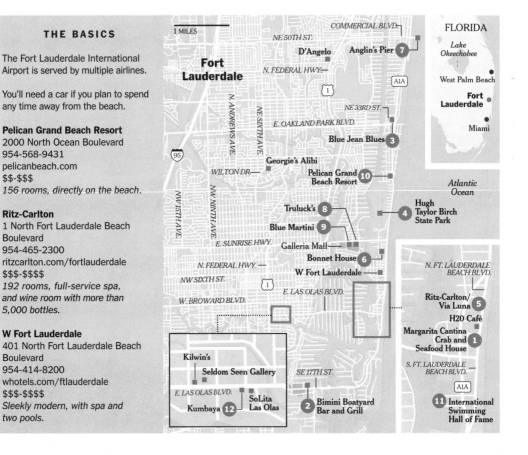

THE BASICS

The Fort Lauderdale International Airport is served by multiple airlines.

You'll need a car if you plan to spend any time away from the beach.

Pelican Grand Beach Resort
2000 North Ocean Boulevard
954-568-9431
pelicanbeach.com
$$-$$$
156 rooms, directly on the beach.

Ritz-Carlton
1 North Fort Lauderdale Beach Boulevard
954-465-2300
ritzcarlton.com/fortlauderdale
$$$-$$$$
192 rooms, full-service spa, and wine room with more than 5,000 bottles.

W Fort Lauderdale
401 North Fort Lauderdale Beach Boulevard
954-414-8200
whotels.com/ftlauderdale
$$$-$$$$
Sleekly modern, with spa and two pools.

South Beach
Miami

South Beach, that trendiest stretch of Miami Beach, Florida, gets a lot of abuse from residents. Too much cologne, critics say; too expensive, too crowded. But like other American meccas of decadence, SoBe still has an irresistible, democratic pull. For everyone from the pale Iowa retiree to the Bentley-driving rapper, it remains the place to strut shamelessly. And even jaded locals still indulge. They may not be taking photos. And perhaps they'll be dressed a bit more casually. But bet on this: They're checking in with the classics and keeping up with the latest trends like everyone else — except they don't need to flaunt it.
— BY DAMIEN CAVE

FRIDAY

1 *On the Boardwalk* 5 p.m.

The beach never gets old. For the timeless South Beach experience, amble along to the wooden boardwalk that extends from 21st to 47th Street before city planners can replace the raised platform with a ground-level path. Take in the views: on one side is the ocean; on the other, the crumbling, yet-to-be-renovated Art Deco hotels that offer a Pompeii-like look back at Miami Beach when diving boards and peach walls still dominated. Then dive into the present at the rooftop pool at the **Gansevoort South** (2377 Collins Avenue; 305-604-1000; gansevoortmiamibeach.com). Sip a SoBe Carnival (cachaça, pineapple juice, and muddled basil) and enjoy the views of either the ocean or the party people.

2 *Music, Not Dancing* 7 p.m.

House. Salsa. Hip-hop. South Beach has many soundtracks, but few musical institutions here are as beloved as the **New World Symphony** (500 17th Street; 305-673-3330; nws.edu), an orchestral academy founded by Michael Tilson Thomas, music director of the San Francisco Symphony. Providing mixed-media extravaganzas one night, free student concerts the next, it manages to be both high-brow

OPPOSITE A cruise ship glides past South Pointe, the southern tip of South Beach.

RIGHT Frolicking at the rooftop pool and bar of the Gansevoort South hotel.

and accessible. You won't find it hard to locate the symphony's new home, designed by Frank Gehry and just a block north of its old location in the Art Deco Lincoln Theater.

3 *Designer Excursion* 9 p.m.

You could follow the herd to **Prime Italian** (101 Ocean Drive; 305-695-8484; primeitalianmiami.com), where Kobe meatballs are a specialty. But lighter, slow-food fare (at better prices) can be found across Biscayne Bay at **Fratelli Lyon** (4141 Northeast Second Avenue; 305-572-2901; fratellilyon.com). Just the fresh cheeses and artisanal olive oil make it worth the trip. Plus, you'll leave with energy to dance. So go straight to the **Florida Room** at Delano (1685 Collins Avenue; 305-674-6152; delano-hotel.com), where on most Fridays Angela Laino belts out funk and soul backed by a band rich with brass.

SATURDAY

4 *Sandy Stretch* 7 a.m.

In the 10-plus years that October Rose (yes, a real person) has offered yoga on South Beach (yogasouthbeach.org), it has become a 365-day-a-year institution. Sometimes there are as many as 20 people near the usual lifeguard stand at Third Street, each donating about $5. All that locust posing will make you hungry, so afterward head to **A La Folie** (516 Espanola Way; 305-538-4484; alafoliecafe.com; $), a hidden French gem, for a butter-sugar crepe with a cappuccino.

5 *Vintage and Vixens* 11 a.m.

Sure, you could buy something new. The malls would love you for it. But why not be both cool and conservationist by going consignment? **Fly Boutique** (650 Lincoln Road; 305-604-8508; flyboutiquevintage.com) is overflowing with few-of-a-kind items, from Emilio Pucci scarves for less than $100 to classic Levi's and even Louis Vuitton luggage large enough for a move to Europe (though the trunk will cost you $1,495). **Beatnix** (1149 Washington Avenue; 305-532-8733; beatnixmiami.com) offers a costume-centric mix, heavy on the polyester. It's also where

South Beach's vixen bartenders buy their get-ups. For $149, Beatnix will make a corset-tutu combo.

6 *Read Your Lunch* 1 p.m.

Miamians sometimes joke that their most popular independent bookseller — **Books and Books** — should be renamed Book and Book because of how little residents read. Regardless, the food and service at its South Beach cafe (927 Lincoln Road; 305-532-3222; booksandbooks.com; $$) are as consistent as Carl Hiaasen's sense of humor. The Key West crab cakes are rich in flavor, but not too heavy, and the homemade cupcakes and Illy espresso might explain why Malcolm Gladwell and other writers spend hours lollygagging at the outdoor tables. Or maybe it really is the books.

7 *Fore!* 3 p.m.

Now it's time for some brawn. Try hitting a large bucket of balls at **Miami Beach Golf Club** (2301 Alton Road; 305-532-3350; miamibeachgolfclub.com). As you hook your drive toward the not-so-distant Atlantic, try to imagine the view in 1923, when the course opened, or during World War II, when the Army rented the course for $1 a day and tossed smoke grenades all over the greens.

LEFT Mac's Club Deuce is a classic dive bar.

8 *Go Gatsby* 8 p.m.

Travel back in time again. First stop, the **Betsy Hotel** (1440 Ocean Drive; 305-531-6100; thebetsyhotel.com), newly renovated to capture an old-fashioned charm that flappers could appreciate —especially in the surrounding sea of neon. The hotel's restaurant, **BLT Steak** (305-673-0044; bltsteak.com; $$$$), part of the upscale steakhouse chain, essentially sits in the lobby. All the better for watching the wealthy and established mix with the young and skimpy. The popovers and aged beef aren't bad either, though prices are best forgotten in a drunken haze.

9 *Highs and Lows* 11 p.m.

Remember when the villains of *Goldfinger* cheated at cards, or when Tony Montana in *Scarface* declared "This is paradise" by the pool? It was at the **Fontainebleau** (4441 Collins Avenue; 305-538-2000;

fontainebleau.com). And after a $1 billion renovation, the FB is back. If you can get past the velvet rope, sashay downstairs into **Liv**, the hotel nightclub where weekends usually include a big celebrity (Jennifer Lopez was one example). If that fails, drink martinis in the lobby, designed by Morris Lapidus, which was also restored. The famous bowtie-tile floors remain, as does the staircase to nowhere, designed solely for grand entrances. Finish the night down to earth, with some cheap beer and pool at **Mac's Club Deuce** (222 14th Street; 305-531-6200), a classic dive bar that draws drunks, drag queens, cops, and traveling executives.

OPPOSITE ABOVE Inside at the Betsy Hotel, renovated but with a charm that flappers could appreciate.

BELOW An early-morning yoga class on the beach with instructor October Rose.

SUNDAY

10 *The Deep End* 9 a.m.

South Pointe Park, at the tip of South Beach, has been treated to a $22 million facelift, and while it looks fantastic, some of the best sights are in the water. The water right off the pier is a great place for snorkeling, surfing, or fishing, with stingrays, bright tropical fish, and lots of colorful locals. You can rent a full snorkeling package for $20 a day at **Tarpoon Dive Center** (300 Alton Road; 305-532-1445; tarpoondivecenter.com).

11 *Soak and Go* Noon

Reliable regeneration can be found with brunch and a good spa cleansing at the **Standard Hotel** (40 Island Avenue; 305-673-1717; standardhotels.com), a 1920s motor lodge that André Balazs turned into a holistic oasis a few years ago. If you don't want to spring for a massage, try the much cheaper alternative of soaking in a scented private tub overlooking Biscayne Bay. Finish up by the pool with an ahi tuna niçoise salad and an Arnold Palmer — that would be half lemonade, half iced tea for all you non-Floridians.

ABOVE The newly refurbished South Pointe Park.

OPPOSITE SoundScape, a park just outside the new Frank Gehry-designed home of the New World Symphony.

THE BASICS

Fly to Miami International Airport and take a cab or shuttle to South Beach. Get around on foot and by cab.

W South Beach
2201 Collins Avenue
305-938-3000
wsouthbeach.com
$$$$
Among the swankiest of several new hotels.

The Gansevoort South
2377 Collins Avenue
305-604-1000
gansevoortmiamibeach.com
$$$$
The enormous pools are a highlight.

The Fontainebleau
4441 Collins Avenue
305-538-2000
fontainebleau.com
$$$$
Recapturing former glory after a $1 billion renovation.

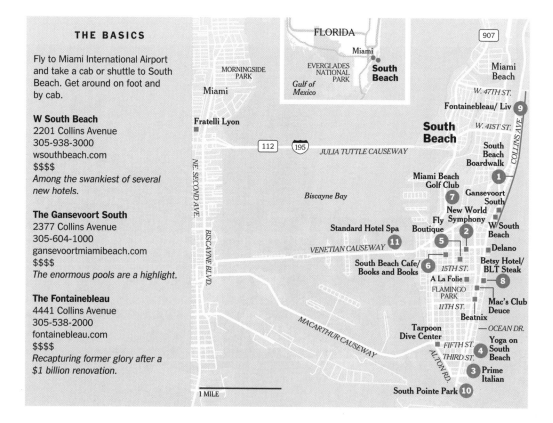

Cuban Miami

Cuban culture is as integral to the colorful fabric of Miami as the palm tree. One could be easily forgiven, in fact, for forgetting that the city's most ubiquitous import from Cuba — the cafecito window, where locals of all persuasions converge to down tiny shots of strong, sugary coffee — has not been a fixture here for as long as the sand or the Florida sun. Other elements play the same tricks on the mind, from minty mojitos to those boxy guayabera shirts, making it a challenge to spend even a few hours in Miami without experiencing at least a hint of its Cuban accent. But it's certainly possible to dig deeper, to be immersed in ways so distilled — through a host of nightclubs, cafes, museums, and galleries — that you could forget that you have not left the United States.
— BY BETH GREENFIELD

FRIDAY

1 *Miami's Ellis Island* 4 p.m.

The **Freedom Tower** (600 Biscayne Boulevard; 305-237-7700), a butter-yellow beacon in downtown Miami, served as an immigration processing center

OPPOSITE Biscayne Bay from the water's edge at Ermita de la Caridad, a shrine to displaced Cubans.

BELOW Watch the cigars being rolled at El Credito Cigar Factory, in the heart of Little Havana.

for more than 400,000 Cubans in the 1960s; today it's a National Historic Landmark that's owned by Miami-Dade College. During special exhibits, which the college holds here regularly (check mdc.edu for a schedule), you can step inside and gaze up at the 40-foot New World Mural, a twice-restored version of the 1925 original, depicting Ponce de Leon and the Tequesta chief standing before a map of the New World. But even if it's closed, the inspiring Spanish Renaissance Revival-style structure is worth a drive-by.

2 *A Banana Republic* 7 p.m.

There's another mural in the family-style dining room at **Islas Canarias** (285 Northwest 27th Avenue; 305-649-0440; islascanariasrestaurant.com; $$) — this one splashy and music-themed, with images of Cuban stars like Celia Cruz and Tito Puente playing in one big fantasy band. But the food is what really sings here; settle in for traditional specialties like Cuban-style pork chops, ropa vieja (shredded, spiced flank steak), or grilled sirloin, all served with the omnipresent sides of rice, yuca, and sweet plantains.

3 *For a Song* 10 p.m.

Have a heart-thumping live-music experience at **Hoy Como Ayer** (2212 Southwest 8th Street; 305-541-2631; hoycomoayer.us), a diminutive club in the legendary Little Havana neighborhood. (The club's name translates to Today as Yesterday.) You'll find a fired-up crowd decked out in suits, guayaberas, and slinky dresses, awaiting Cuban performers like Malena Burke or Amaury Gutierrez and nibbling on tapas of cheese cubes and tostones, served, cleverly, in cigar boxes. If the night is right you'll catch a show by Miami's own exile music queen, Albita Rodríguez, known simply as Albita. During one such performance there, between explosive numbers, she sang a passionate tribute: "Que culpa tengo yo de estas caderas? Que culpa tengo yo de este sabor? Que culpa tengo yo de haber nacido en Cuba?" ("What fault of mine are these hips? What fault of mine is this flavor? What fault of it is mine that I was born in Cuba?") By the end of the song, the entire house had joined in, erupting with extra gusto along with the final chant of "Cuba! Cuba!" punctuated by Albita's fist pumping into the air.

SATURDAY

4 *When Pressed* 9 a.m.

Enriqueta's (186 Northeast 29th Street; 305-573-4681; $), a bright orange family-owned diner, is a festive island on a gritty stretch in the city's Wynwood district. And it offers a delicious, traditional way to start your day — with a plantain omelet, guava empanada, mamey batido (shake), or even a medianoche, a pressed sandwich of roast pork, ham, cheese, and pickles on egg bread. Pair any option, of course, with a steaming café con leche.

5 *Eighth Is Enough* 11 a.m.

Though the majority of Cubans now live elsewhere in the region, Little Havana is still the symbolic heart of Cuban Miami. And the best starting place for an infusion of culture is its slightly scruffy, well-trafficked stretch of Southwest Eighth Street between 17th and 27th Avenues, known as **Calle Ocho**. It's defined by aromatic cigar and coffee shops, a perpetual blare of salsa trumpets wafting from the distance, and the domino and chess games of older men who gather daily in tiny **Maximo Gómez Park**. Explore a dozen or so Latin-art galleries, including **Molina Fine Art** (1634 Southwest 8th Street; 305-642-0444; molinaartgallery.com) and shops like **El Credito Cigar Factory** (1100 Southwest 8th Street; 305-324-0445; elcreditocigars.com), where you can watch cigars being rolled; **Los Pinareños Fruteria** (1334 Southwest 8th Street; 305-285-1135), the place to get a smooth green coconut pierced with a straw; and **El Pub** (1548 Southwest 8th Street; 305-642-9942), decorated with chicken statuary and known for its café con leche. On a nearby stretch of brick sidewalk, a local Walk of Fame pays tribute to entertainment figures including Gloria Estefan and Maria Conchito Alonso.

6 *Where the Past Is Present* 1 p.m.

Around the corner from the Calle Ocho bustle you'll find the small and quiet **Bay of Pigs Museum** (1821 Southwest Ninth Street; 305-649-4719), a cramped collection of memorabilia, writings, and photos honoring the felled 2506 Brigade of 1961. It puts the neighborhood in immediate political context — as does the **Cuban Memorial Boulevard**, a few blocks north on Southwest 13th Avenue, with its 2506 Brigade memorial, a brass relief of Cuba, and a bust of the 19th-century Cuban poet and freedom fighter Jose Martí. A beautiful ceiba tree here receives offerings from Santeria worshipers, its giant roots pressing up out of the earth like rough-skinned dinosaur claws.

7 *Art and Soul* 5 p.m.

For an impressive array of even more visual art, head to nearby Coral Gables, where the airy **Cernuda Arte** (4155 Ponce de Leon Boulevard; 305-461-1050; cernudaarte.com) gallery shows work strictly by Cubans. Its 25-year-old inventory ranges from colonial to modern masters, and exhibits have featured artists like the painter Tomás Sánchez, the mixed-media artist Flora Fong, and the painter César Santos, whose still-life works and intimate portraits resemble striking, brightly lit photographs.

8 *Waterfront Dining* 7 p.m.

Tucked along the edge of the narrow Miami River, **Garcia's** (398 Northwest North River Drive;

ABOVE El Pub in Calle Ocho, decorated with chicken statuary and known for its café con leche.

BELOW Cigars in the final curing process get the once-over at El Credito Cigar Factory.

305-375-0765; garciasmiami.com; $$) is a downtown Miami seafood joint that's a longtime favorite for its super-fresh catches and reasonable prices and for the warm, friendly vibe of the Garcia brothers, fishermen who left Cuba in the late '60s to begin new lives here. Enjoy a plate of grouper, yellow rice, and sweet plantains, plus a glowing view of Miami's skyline.

SUNDAY

9 *A Spiritual Moment* 10 a.m.

Have a contemplative morning on the shores of Biscayne Bay at the **Ermita de la Caridad** (3609 South Miami Avenue, Coconut Grove; 305-854-2404; ermitadelacaridad.org). It's a tepee-shaped shrine to displaced Cubans, with a Catholic chapel featuring a striking sepia mural of exiles' struggles.

10 *New Squeeze* Noon

By now you've most likely realized that mealtimes are a huge part of Cuban culture. Get your last licks at **El Palacio de los Jugos** in West Miami (5721 West Flagler Street; 305-264-8662; $), an unassuming produce-stand–type market that doles out tasty Cuban tamales, grilled pork, and fresh juices from tropical fruits like papaya and mamey. You'll have to elbow your way through the Sunday mobs to snag a spot at one of the few al fresco tables, but it's well worth it—for the food as well as the scene.

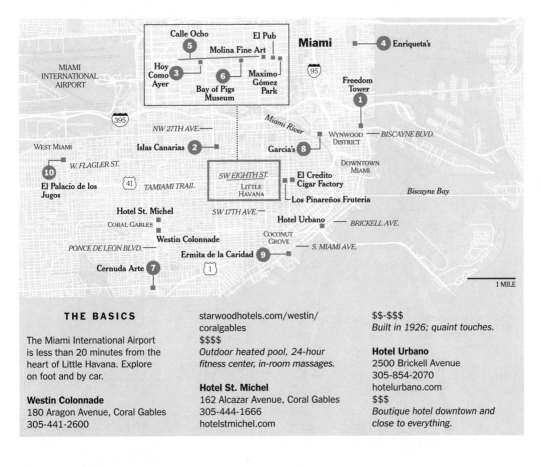

THE BASICS

The Miami International Airport is less than 20 minutes from the heart of Little Havana. Explore on foot and by car.

Westin Colonnade
180 Aragon Avenue, Coral Gables
305-441-2600

starwoodhotels.com/westin/coralgables
$$$$
Outdoor heated pool, 24-hour fitness center, in-room massages.

Hotel St. Michel
162 Alcazar Avenue, Coral Gables
305-444-1666
hotelstmichel.com

$$-$$$
Built in 1926; quaint touches.

Hotel Urbano
2500 Brickell Avenue
305-854-2070
hotelurbano.com
$$$
Boutique hotel downtown and close to everything.

The Everglades

Not quite the brackish swamp that many imagine it to be, the vast south Florida wetland known as the Everglades is actually a clear, wide, shallow river that flows like molasses. And living within its million-plus acres are 200 types of fish, 350 species of birds, and 120 different kinds of trees, just for starters, all less than an hour south of Miami. Of course, to see the iridescent-winged purple gallinule, breaching bottlenose dolphins, and still alligators soaking in the sun, you have to be willing to stop and slow down, moving as languidly as the River of Grass itself. Luckily, the availability of ranger programs and self-guided tours means you needn't be an expert hiker or kayaker to get below the surface of this beautiful, tangled landscape. — BY BETH GREENFIELD

FRIDAY

1 *Under the Boardwalk* 2 p.m.

To hang with more creatures than you can count, head into the **Everglades National Park**'s main **Ernest F. Coe** entrance (305-242-7700; nps.gov/ever/planyourvisit/visitorcenters.htm), near Homestead. You'll find winding boardwalks like the Anhinga Trail, named for the majestic water bird that stands with wings stretched wide to dry its black and white feathers in the sun. A stroll will likely reveal several anhingas, plus green and tri-colored herons, red-bellied turtles, double-crested cormorants, and many alligators. Don't miss the striking Pa-hay-okee Overlook, a short and steep walkway that juts out over a dreamily endless field of billowing, wheat-colored sawgrass.

2 *Pleasure Cruise* 4:45 p.m.

Pick up maps at the Coe entrance and then head deeper west in the park to the **Flamingo Visitor Center** (239-695-2945), where a small, quiet tour boat (evergladesnationalparkboattoursflamingo.com) whisks passengers from the close wetlands of the park out into the glimmering, airy expanse of the Florida Bay. In just under two hours, you'll get a narrated tour, glimpses of elegant water birds (perhaps the great white heron or roseate spoonbill), and a glorious, multicolored sunset over the water.

3 *Search for Tamale* 7:30 p.m.

There's nothing much going on in Homestead, the scruffy town that borders the park's eastern entrance, but a small collection of Mexican restaurants serving tasty eats on North Krome Avenue ensures that you'll at least be well fed. **Casita Tejas** (27 North Krome Avenue, Homestead; 305-248-8224; casitatejas.com; $) offers authentic offerings like beef gorditas, chicken tamales, and chile rellenos in a homey, festive atmosphere.

SATURDAY

4 *Exotic Produce* 8 a.m.

Start your morning off with a thick, fresh-fruit milkshake at **Robert Is Here** (19200 Southwest 344th Street, Homestead; 305-246-1592; robertishere.com), a family-run farm stand offering papayas, star fruits, kumquats, guavas, sapodillas, mameys, and other tropical treats among heaps of fresh oranges and grapefruits.

5 *In the Loop* 10 a.m.

Along the northern rim of the national park you will find the **Shark Valley** entrance (Route 41, Tamiami Trail; 305-221-8776), where a paved loop is traversable by foot, bicycle, or guided tram ride

OPPOSITE Big Cypress National Preserve.

RIGHT Boardwalks in the swamps of Everglades National Park are vantage points for seeing alligators, turtles, and a multicolored profusion of water-loving birds.

and is often host to sleepy crocs or gators. (The Everglades is the only place in the world where alligators, which live in fresh water, and saltwater crocodiles live side by side.) The two-hour tram ride, led by a naturalist, is the best option for coping with the heat and the mosquitoes, which peak here between June and October. It will pause halfway through to let you climb to the top of a 45-foot-high observation deck affording 20-mile wilderness views in all directions.

6 *Swamp Things* 1 p.m.

Just north of the Everglades National Park is the **Big Cypress National Preserve** (nps.gov/bicy) — a tract that narrowly escaped being developed as Miami's international airport in the 1970s. And within its borders lies a novel opportunity for those who prefer to explore this region on foot: ranger-led swamp hikes that set off from the **Oasis Visitor Center** (52105 Tamiami Trail East, Ochopee). "From the highway, all you see is brown and green," noted ranger Corinne Fenner, leading people into the thigh-deep waters of cypress-tree stands. "It's nice to get out into the prairie and notice all the colors."

BELOW Take a ranger-led hike in water that looks surprisingly clean and feels deliciously cool on a hot day.

And the hues you'll see are certainly magical: the butter yellow of the Everglades daisy, bright violet of nettle-leaf velvetberry flowers, electric lime of freshwater sponges, and deep scarlet of a red-bellied woodpecker. The water itself — which collects in a sandy peat and limestone basin, helping silvery bald cypress trees thrive — looks shockingly clear and feels deliciously cool soaking through jeans and sneakers.

7 *Drive-Thru Wilderness* 3:30 p.m.

A Big Cypress driving tour, north of the Gulf Coast canoe launch on the gravel Turner River Road, offers various close-up encounters with wildlife. Along the scenic 17-mile route, you're sure to rub elbows with creeping turtles, nesting ospreys, and clusters of the alligators that like to float lazily in the narrow creeks here, leaving nothing but steely eyes and snouts above water.

8 *Stuffed Animals, Stuffed Belly* 6 p.m.

Not for the faint of heart when it comes to pushing carnivorous limits, the **Rod and Gun Club**, in the small fishing village of Everglades City (200 West Broadway; 239-695-2100; evergladesrodandgun.com; $$), is a handsome, historic riverside inn where you can unwind from your full day of touring with a hearty dinner. Swamp and Turf (steak and frogs legs) and gator nuggets are among the eclectic offerings. Afterward, have a cocktail in the cozy lounge, where you can shoot pool under the eerie double gaze of a gator skin and deer head, both mounted on the wall.

SUNDAY

9 *Paddle Your Own Canoe* 10 a.m.

The southwest edge of the park sits at the precipice of glistening Chokoloskee Bay and the Ten Thousand Islands area — a pristine region of mangroves and sandy keys mostly reachable only by boat via the 99-mile Wilderness Waterway canoe and kayak trail. While experienced paddlers can plunge right into a days-long journey, camping on raised "chickee" platforms or sand spits along the way, beginners are best off joining one of the many shorter, organized trips on more navigable creeks, like the one led weekly by national park naturalists, leaving from the park's **Gulf Coast Visitor Center**

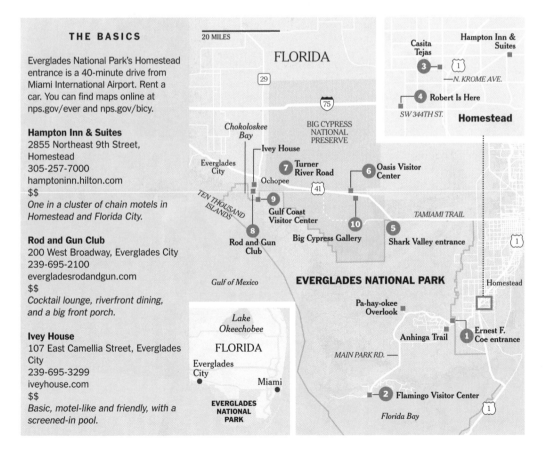

(815 Oyster Bar Lane, Everglades City). "I never get tired of this area," a naturalist, Brian Ettling, said during one such four-hour journey, leading canoeists single file beneath a cathedral of arching mangrove branches. He excitedly pointed out blue herons, jumping mullet fish, and skittish tree crabs. He gave lessons on the hunting habits of swooping turkey vultures, which have a sense of smell rivaling a bloodhound's, and on the hip attributes of screechy red-shouldered hawks: "They're like the local punk rockers. They eat lizards and scream."

10 *Caught on Film* 3 p.m.
On your way back east along the Tamiami Trail, be sure to stop and visit the **Big Cypress Gallery**

(52388 Tamiami Trail, Ochopee; 239-695-2428; clydebutcher.com). Here, photographer Clyde Butcher's large-format, black and white landscapes perfectly capture the romantic essence of this swampland and put your own fresh experiences into striking artistic perspective.

ABOVE Wild beauty at sunset in the Big Cypress National Preserve.

THE BASICS

Everglades National Park's Homestead entrance is a 40-minute drive from Miami International Airport. Rent a car. You can find maps online at nps.gov/ever and nps.gov/bicy.

Hampton Inn & Suites
2855 Northeast 9th Street, Homestead
305-257-7000
hamptoninn.hilton.com
$$
One in a cluster of chain motels in Homestead and Florida City.

Rod and Gun Club
200 West Broadway, Everglades City
239-695-2100
evergladesrodandgun.com
$$
Cocktail lounge, riverfront dining, and a big front porch.

Ivey House
107 East Camellia Street, Everglades City
239-695-3299
iveyhouse.com
$$
Basic, motel-like and friendly, with a screened-in pool.

Key West

Key West, haven to artists and writers, chefs and hippies, is somehow more Caribbean than Floridian. The independent-spirited transplants who inhabit it work hard to keep it that way. One-speed bicycles weave their way through colorful village streets crammed with almost as many chickens as cars. Happy hour blends into dinner. And everything is shaped by the ocean, from the fish market-driven menus and the nautical-inspired art to the dawn gatherings of sunrise worshipers and the tipplers' goodbye waves at sunset. Be careful or you might just catch what islanders call "Keys disease" — a sudden desire to cut ties with home and move there.
— BY SARAH WILDMAN

FRIDAY

1 *Two Wheels Are Enough* 4 p.m.

As any self-respecting bohemian local knows, the best way to get around Key West is on a bicycle. Bike rental businesses offer drop-off service to many hotels. Two reliable companies are **Eaton Bikes** (830 Eaton Street; 305-294-8188; eatonbikes.com) and **Re-Cycle** (5160 Overseas Highway; U.S. 1; 305-292-3336; recyclekw.com). Rentals will be around $20 for the first day and half that for each additional. Orient yourself by biking over to the **Truman Annex**, a palm-lined oasis of calm made up of two-story whitewashed buildings that surrounds the **Little White House** (111 Front Street; 305-294-9911; trumanlittlewhitehouse.com), where Harry Truman spent working vacations.

2 *Cleanse the Palate* 7 p.m.

Key West chefs pride themselves on a culinary philosophy of simple cooking and fresh ingredients. A perfect example is the **Flaming Buoy Filet Co.** (1100 Packer Street; 305-295-7970; theflamingbuoy.com; $$), a nouveau seafood restaurant owned and run by two Cincinnati transplants, Fred Isch and his partner, Scot Forste. The 10 rustic wood tables are hand-painted in orange and yellow; the lights are

low and the crowd amiable. This is home-cooking, island style, with dishes like black bean soup swirled with Cheddar cheese, sour cream, and cilantro or the fresh catch of the day served with a broccoli cake and tasty mashed potatoes.

3 *Small World* 9 p.m.

You can't bike a block on this island without bumping into a would-be Gauguin wielding a palette and paintbrush. There's an outsize and vibrant arts scene that's evident at places like **Lucky Street Gallery** (1130 Duval Street; 305-294-3973; luckystreetgallery.com) and the **Gallery on Greene** (606 Greene Street; 305-294-1669; galleryongreene.com). For a warm introduction, head to the Armory, a rifle storage house built in 1903 and recently converted into the **Studios of Key West** (600 White Street; 305-296-0458; tskw.org), an airy, art-filled space with rotating exhibitions, evening folk concerts, talks by artists-in-residence, and drop-in art classes. Expect to find your barista there, and the bike rental guy and the woman who will sell you a T-shirt tomorrow. It's a small town.

4 *Mix It Up* 11 p.m.

While Key West night life has long been synonymous with boozy karaoke and mediocre margaritas, watering holes like the tiny **Orchid Bar** (1004 Duval Street; 305-296-9915; orchidkeyinn.com) are quietly moving in a more sophisticated direction. Bartenders there take mixology seriously. Try the St.-Germain 75, with Hendrick's Gin, St.-Germain, fresh lemon

OPPOSITE A December day at Casa Marina Resort.

RIGHT A Key West sunset. Many of the growing population of islanders moved in after succumbing to what they call "Keys disease," a visitor's sudden desire to stay for good.

juice, and Champagne. This Deco-cool sliver of a space overlooks an illuminated pool and draws a mellow crew.

SATURDAY

5 *Salute the Sun* 8:15 a.m.

Every morning, a dozen spiritual seekers — an eclectic mix including tattooed artists and elementary-school teachers — assemble at Fort Zachary Taylor State Park for **Yoga on the Beach** (305-296-7352; yogaonbeach.com). Nancy Curran and Don Bartolone, yogis from Massachusetts, teach energetic vinyasa-style yoga in a clearing of pines, facing the sea. The $18 drop-in fee includes state park entrance, muslin dropcloths, and yoga mats.

6 *Imports at Breakfast* 11 a.m.

An island of transplants offers plenty to sample from the world over. Craving France? Stop at **La Crêperie Key West** (300 Petronia Street; 305-517-6799; lacreperiekeywest.com; $$), where Yolande Findlay and Sylvie Le Nouail, both Brittany born, serve crepes in an open kitchen. Start with a savory crepe like ratatouille and then move on to something sweet like red velvet with dark Belgian chocolate, strawberries, and English custard. If you feel more like New York, try **Sarabeth's** (530 Simonton Street; 305-293-8181; sarabethskeywest.com; $), a branch of the popular Manhattan brunch spot.

7 *Island Style* 1 p.m.

Just because islanders pride themselves on being casual, do not assume they don't want to look great. **Bésame Mucho** (315 Petronia Street; 305-294-1928; besamemucho.net) is an old-world general store packed with everything from Belgian linen to Dr. Hauschka skin care, to delicate baubles like tiny beaded pyrite necklaces. Across the street is **Wanderlust kw** (310 Petronia Street; 305-509-7065; wanderlustkw.com), stocked with well-priced dresses and whimsical watercolors of Key West houses by

local artists. For swank décor, check out **Jan George Interior Design** (600 Frances Street; 305-509-8449; jangeorge.com), a furniture shop that carries dreamy stark-white couches from the Italian line Gervasoni. The owners, Jan Oostdyk and his spouse, George Rutgers, landed as tourists from the Netherlands and never left.

8 *Drinks at Sunset* 5 p.m.

Skip the hustle of Mallory Square and work your way through the white-tablecloth dining room to **Louie's Backyard Afterdeck Bar** (700 Waddell Avenue; 305-294-1061; louiesbackyard.com), where a large wood-planked patio faces the ocean and the setting sun. A gregarious crowd of artists and New England snowbirds gathers daily. It's like an outdoor Cheers.

9 *Dining on the Duval* 7 p.m.

Since opening in 2002, the restaurant **Nine One Five** (915 Duval Street; 305-296-0669; 915duval.com; $$$) has gotten high marks for its Asian-inspired seafood and ambience — a large white porch that's great for people-watching. Later the owner, Stuart Kemp, turned the second floor into the Point5 lounge, serving smaller bites like grilled snapper tacos

ABOVE Some of the finds at Bésame Mucho, one of multiple shopping options around town.

BELOW Touring by bicycle with Lloyd's Tropical Bike.

and stick-to-your-ribs mac and cheese to a younger crowd. If you linger after dinner, Point5 becomes a party, with D.J. George spinning funk and soul and the island's gay and straight worlds dancing together under filament lights strung outdoors.

10 *Drag Show* 9 p.m.

Drag shows are part of Key West's patrimony. One favorite performer is Randy Roberts, who has performed as Bette Midler, Cher, and Lady Gaga at **La Te Da** (1125 Duval Street; 305-296-6706; lateda.com). After the show, hoof it down to **Porch** (429 Caroline Street, No. 2; 305-517-6358; theporchkw.com), a wine and artisanal beer bar on the luminous first floor of a Victorian mansion, just off Duval.

SUNDAY

11 *Seaworthy Pursuits* Noon

With all the shopping and eating, it is easy to forget why you're really here: to get off the street and onto the water. **Lazy Dog** (5114 Overseas Highway; 305-295-9898; lazydog.com) offers two- and four-hour kayaking or two-hour paddleboard tours through crystal clear coastal waters and into the deep green waterways of the gnarled mangrove forests. Or if you're just looking to dip a toe in the sea, bike over to Clarence S. Higgs Memorial Beach, a strip of sand by the genial beach bar restaurant **Salute!** (1000 Atlantic Boulevard; 305-292-1117; saluteonthebeach.com), rent a beach chair, and kick back.

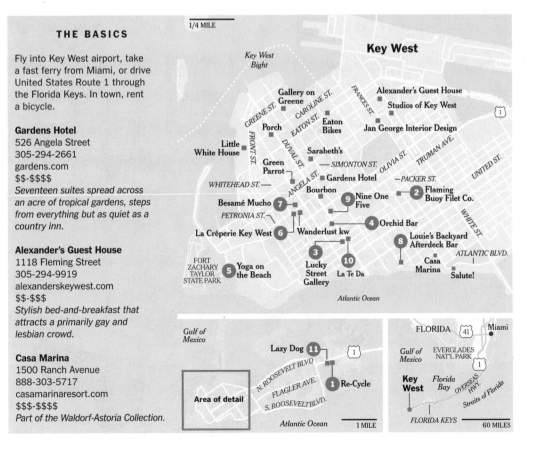

THE BASICS

Fly into Key West airport, take a fast ferry from Miami, or drive United States Route 1 through the Florida Keys. In town, rent a bicycle.

Gardens Hotel
526 Angela Street
305-294-2661
gardens.com
$$-$$$$
Seventeen suites spread across an acre of tropical gardens, steps from everything but as quiet as a country inn.

Alexander's Guest House
1118 Fleming Street
305-294-9919
alexanderskeywest.com
$$-$$$
Stylish bed-and-breakfast that attracts a primarily gay and lesbian crowd.

Casa Marina
1500 Ranch Avenue
888-303-5717
casamarinaresort.com
$$$-$$$$
Part of the Waldorf-Astoria Collection.

Naples

If you filtered all the glitz out of Miami, you'd get Naples, Florida. This small Gulf-side city has a pleasingly anodyne quality that's worlds away from the cosmopolitan bustle found only a two-hour drive due east, on the Atlantic coast. Affluent Midwesterners, who have adopted Naples as a getaway from nasty Northern weather, bring a certain oh-gosh air to town. Don't be surprised if you keep seeing the same faces over and over — these snowbirds might move at a slower pace than the Miami set, but they get around.
— BY TED LOOS

FRIDAY

1 *Sunset Cocktails* 5 p.m.

Cocktail hour is sacred around these parts. As the sun sets, make your way to **Gumbo Limbo**, the beachfront bar and restaurant at the Ritz-Carlton, Naples (280 Vanderbilt Beach Road; 239-598-3300; ritzcarlton.com/naples). Order a Naples Sunset, a fruity rum drink, and follow the dipping sun as the outdoor deck lights up with tiki torches and the laughter of the polo-shirt-wearing crowd.

2 *Well Seasoned* 8 p.m.

Don't go to Naples expecting molecular gastronomy; restaurants play it conservatively. Among the more exciting spots is **Sea Salt** (1186 Third Street South; 239-434-7258; seasaltnaples.com; $$$), a boisterous place that opened in 2008 and has been praised by magazines like *Esquire* for its devotion to local and organic ingredients. The menu prizes bold flavors over razzle-dazzle: buffalo mozzarella salad, well-marbled Wagyu rib-eye. The chef also has a thing for sprinkles: porcini powder, cinnamon salt, and of course sea salt. The wine list roams the globe, with particular attention to Italy.

3 *Early Night Owls* 10 p.m.

Naples will never be known for its night life. But even here, 20-something fans of bottle service can go to **Vision Night Club** (11901 Tamiami Trail North; 239-591-8383; visionniteclub.com), where three rooms with disco balls and colored lights keep the dance floor moving. A mellower vibe can be found at **Avenue Wine Café** (483 Fifth Avenue South; 239-403-9463; avenuewinecafe.com), where

Colin Estrem, the owner, said he catered to "young professionals, not the rich Naples crowd." Inside, patrons sample from 100 wines and about 70 beers on offer. Outside, cigar aficionados puff away on the patio until the wee hours.

SATURDAY

4 *Modern Art* 10 a.m.

The **Naples Museum of Art** (5833 Pelican Bay Boulevard; 239-597-1900; thephil.org) is a small gem, with a permanent collection that has a strong selection of American modernism (including works by Charles Sheeler and Oscar Bluemner) and Mexican modernism (renowned names like Tamayo and Orozco). The senior-citizen docents are lovingly bossy, and not shy about steering visitors toward what they consider the best views.

5 *Million-Dollar Beach* 11:30 a.m.

When the sun is strong, Neapolitans hit the beach. Don't set up camp near the town pier at Fifth Street South — it's too crowded. Ditto for anything along the northern end — too many hotels. For a spot that's just right, head south toward 18th

OPPOSITE Mosaic tile work by Roberto Burle Marx in the Brazilian Garden at the Naples Botanical Garden.

BELOW When the sun is strong, Neapolitans hit the beach, open to the public even in front of the mansions.

Avenue South, the last downtown street with direct beach access. (Parking can be scarce, so bring a pocketful of quarters and try nearby Gordon Drive.) With flip-flops in hand, a short walk south offers privacy. It also induces real estate envy. Some of Naples's plushest over-the-top mansions are along this stretch of beach, exposed to prying eyes.

6 *Jolly Good* 2 p.m.

A faithful adherence to classic pub fare draws a loyal crowd to the **Jolly Cricket** (720 Fifth Avenue South; 239-304-9460; thejollycricket.com; $$), which opened last year along the city's main drag. Ceiling fans and wicker chairs set the mood. At night there's even a standards-playing pianist, complete with brandy snifter for tips. The kitchen turns out a succulent fish 'n chips served with housemade tartar sauce.

7 *Dress Up* 4 p.m.

Downtown shopping favors women's clothing and accessories. Some of the best shops are concentrated on Third Street South. **Marissa Collections** (No. 1167; 239-263-4333; marissacollections.com), a high-fashion fixture, has added mini-boutiques for Oscar de la Renta and a men's line from the designer Brunello Cucinelli. Another good retail cluster lines Fifth Avenue South. Stop by **Seraphim Boutique** (No. 600, Suite 106; 239-261-8494; seraphimboutique.com), where Tanya Anderson, the owner, specializes in flirty, fun resort wear—the kind of thing you'd pick up on a vacation, like a Luna Luz tie-dyed halter dress.

8 *Sigh and Meditate* 6 p.m.

Until recently, spas weren't as prominent as Naples's luxe reputation would suggest. So the arrival a few years ago of a **Golden Door** spa (475 Seagate Drive; 239-594-6321; goldendoor.com/naples) was a cause for celebration—and a new reason for a trip here. Situated at the Naples Grande Resort, the 16,000-square-foot spa is filled with Asian-inflected details like bamboo groves and teak trim. In addition to

the sauna and whirlpool, there's a meditation labyrinth where you can unwind after an avocado-citrus wrap.

9 *French Provincial* 8 p.m.

A sweet little bistro tucked onto a side street downtown, **Bleu Provence** (1234 Eighth Street South; 239-261-8239; bleuprovencenaples.com; $$$) is done up as a farmhouse dining room and really feels as if you could be in the hills above Nice. Escargot, moules-frites, foie gras, loup de mer, tarte aux oignons—there's plenty of French to go on. After dinner, wander down to the dock to see if the pelicans are still awake.

SUNDAY

10 *Bring a Racquet* 10 a.m.

The thunking of tennis balls is heard everywhere in Naples, but most of the courts are sequestered behind hedges in high-end condo developments. That makes the **Arthur L. Allen Tennis Center** (735 Eighth Street South; 239-213-3060; allentenniscenter.com),

ABOVE Marissa Collections is a 10,000-square-foot bastion of luxury that sells designer fashion.

BELOW The Naples Museum of Art, a small gem with a strong selection of American and Mexican modernism.

in downtown's quiet Cambier Park, all the more inviting. The 12 Har-Tru courts are as well kept as a private club's, but for an affordable fee, anyone can play. There's a sign-up board to help you find pick-up games at your level (blue cards for men, pink ones for ladies).

11 *Lush Vegetation* 1 p.m.

Beaches are great, but a slightly more educational way to experience Naples's balmy climate is found at the dramatically expanded and renovated **Naples Botanical Garden** (4820 Bayshore Drive; 239-643-7275; naplesgarden.org), which focuses on subtropical flora. Lush Caribbean and Brazilian gardens are perfectly manicured, and the Children's

Garden features a tiny herb patch and spraying fountains. The colorful butterfly house draws the most visitors, and as you look for the elusive electric-blue variety, you may run into that well-dressed couple you dined next to the previous evening. Par for the course in Naples.

ABOVE The Children's Garden at the Naples Botanical Garden has a boardwalk, an herb patch, and fountains.

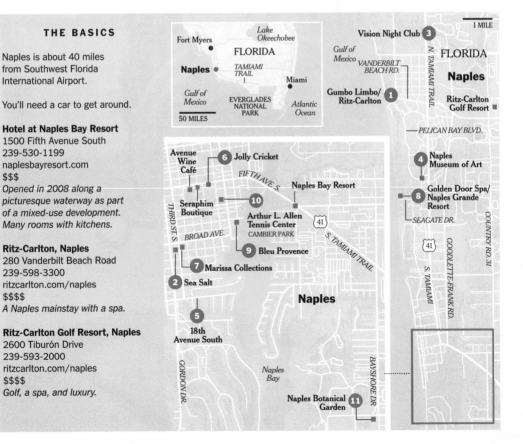

THE BASICS

Naples is about 40 miles from Southwest Florida International Airport.

You'll need a car to get around.

Hotel at Naples Bay Resort
1500 Fifth Avenue South
239-530-1199
naplesbayresort.com
$$$
Opened in 2008 along a picturesque waterway as part of a mixed-use development. Many rooms with kitchens.

Ritz-Carlton, Naples
280 Vanderbilt Beach Road
239-598-3300
ritzcarlton.com/naples
$$$$
A Naples mainstay with a spa.

Ritz-Carlton Golf Resort, Naples
2600 Tiburón Drive
239-593-2000
ritzcarlton.com/naples
$$$$
Golf, a spa, and luxury.

1 MILE

Fort Myers

Lake Okeechobee

FLORIDA

Naples
TAMIAMI TRAIL

Miami

Gulf of Mexico

EVERGLADES NATIONAL PARK

Atlantic Ocean

50 MILES

Vision Night Club 3

Gulf of Mexico VANDERBILT BEACH RD.

Gumbo Limbo/ Ritz-Carlton 1

N. TAMIAMI TRAIL

FLORIDA

Naples

Ritz-Carlton Golf Resort

— PELICAN BAY BLVD.

Avenue Wine Café

6 Jolly Cricket

FIFTH AVE. S.

Naples Bay Resort

4 Naples Museum of Art

Seraphim Boutique

10

Arthur L. Allen Tennis Center 41
CAMBIER PARK

8 Golden Door Spa/ Naples Grande Resort

SEAGATE DR.

THIRD ST. S.

BROAD AVE.

9 Bleu Provence

41

7 Marissa Collections

2 Sea Salt

Naples

S. TAMIAMI TRAIL

S. TAMIAMI

GOODLETTE-FRANK RD.

COUNTRY RD. 31

5

18th Avenue South

GORDON DR.

Naples Bay

Naples Botanical Garden 11

BAYSHORE DR

Atlanta

First, don't call it Hotlanta anymore. It's the ATL, the code for the teeming airport that is a fitting emblem for a city so transient it barely recognizes itself, where more than half the adult population is from somewhere else, and where every urban fad, from underground parking to savory ice cream, is embraced. A corporate stronghold, a Southern belle, and a hip-hop capital, Atlanta has wrestled with identity confusion, trying out several slogans in the past few years, from a hip-hop-accompanied "Every Day Is an Opening Day" to a blander "City Lights, Southern Nights." Major civic investments like a grandiose $220 million aquarium, a significant expansion of the High Museum of Art by the architect Renzo Piano, and the purchase of the papers of the Rev. Dr. Martin Luther King Jr. add up to a high tide of enthusiasm, even in a city where optimism is liberally indulged. — BY SHAILA DEWAN

FRIDAY

1 *Tastes of the Town* 5:30 p.m.

Few places can be said to be definitively Atlantan, but the **Colonnade** (1879 Cheshire Bridge Road NE; 404-874-5642; colonnadeatl.com; $) is one: a meat-and-three restaurant with a full bar (rare) and a sizable gay clientele (more rare). The resulting mix is spectacular: black fingernails, Sansabelt trousers, birthday tiaras, Hawaiian shirts, all in a buzzing carpeted dining room with efficiently friendly waiters. When it comes to ordering, stick to the classics: a Bloody Mary to start, fried chicken with yeasty dinner rolls straight from the school cafeteria, and the day's pie.

2 *Old-Time Steps* 7:20 p.m.

Though it sounds vaguely revolutionary, contra dancing is a folk tradition that involves following instructions from a caller, like square-dancing. If the notion of trying this in public gives you qualms, remember that 1) the likelihood of being seen by someone you know is low and 2) the tolerance quotient, at a weekly event where men have been known to show up wearing skirts to keep cool, is high. Show up at the **Clarkston Community Center** (3701 College Avenue, Clarkston) before 7:20 p.m. for basic lessons by the Chattahoochee County Dancers (770-939-8646; contradance.org), and then, when the dance begins at 8, swing your partner (you can easily find one there) to live old-time bands with names like Jump in the Skillet and Cattywampus. Wear soft-soled shoes, or boogie in your socks.

3 *Where Heads Spin* 10:30 p.m.

Since you're already dizzy, visit the **Sun Dial**, the revolving bar atop the Westin hotel (210 Peachtree Street; 404-589-7506; sundialrestaurant.com), where young Atlantans come for the throwback cool and occasional exhibitions of local art. Sip an Atlanta Hurricane (it's in the colada-daiquiri family and arrives in a souvenir glass) or a chocolate martini as you orient yourself with a glittery panoramic view of downtown, the Georgia Dome, CNN's headquarters, and the Georgia Aquarium.

4 *On a Roll* 11:30 p.m.

Roller-skating is an integral part of hip-hop culture in Atlanta, which is home to OutKast, Usher, and Young Jeezy, among other stars. Beyoncé had her 21st birthday party at the Cascade roller rink here, and Dallas Austin paid homage to the flawless moves of

OPPOSITE The Atlanta Cyclorama and Civil War Museum. Inside is a panoramic painting of the Battle of Atlanta.

RIGHT Smooth moves at the Golden Glide rink. Roller skating is an integral part of Atlanta hip-hop culture.

skate dancers in his film *The ATL*. On Friday nights, the virtuosos descend on **Golden Glide** (2750 Wesley Chapel Road in Decatur, but it's tucked behind a shopping strip; 404-288-7773; atlantarollerskating.com) for adult skate, where posses practice their smooth moves until the wee hours. If you haven't been practicing, skate inside the green line for your own safety. Or just stay on the sideline and gawk.

SATURDAY

5 *Robust Start* Noon

You had a late night, so take your time getting to **Watershed** (406 West Ponce de Leon Avenue, Decatur; 404-378-4900; watershedrestaurant.com; $$), a gas station converted into an airy Southern restaurant. Reservations are recommended, and child-tolerance is required, but the chicken hash with griddle cakes and poached eggs is worth the bother.

6 *A Little Shopping* 1:30 p.m.

After brunch, browse the chic specialty shops near the main square of Decatur, the city-suburb that has won praise for its sensitive take on urban revitalization. One favorite is **Mingei World Arts** (427 Church Street; 404-371-0101; mingeiworldarts.com), an import store with a sense of humor, which offers items like vintage Bollywood posters or baskets woven from telephone wire. For the designer chef there's **Taste** (416 Church Street; 404-370-1863; tastedecatur.com), with two-handed Dumbo cups and vintage-print aprons.

7 *War on Canvas* 3:30 p.m.

When Gen. John A. Logan was considering a run for vice president in the 1880s, he commissioned a political ad in the form of a giant painting of the Battle of Atlanta, in which he for a time commanded the Army of the Tennessee for the Union. The work, billed as the world's largest oil painting, is now housed in **Grant Park**, in a circular room not unlike a planetarium, and viewed from a rotating bank of seats (**Atlanta Cyclorama and Civil War Museum**; 800 Cherokee Avenue; 404-624-1071; bcaatlanta. com). It is accompanied by a taped narration, a good way to get your requisite dose of Civil War history. A diorama was added in the 1930s, which sounds like a terrible idea until you see how seamlessly it blends into the painting, or notice a replica of Clark Gable as a dead Yankee. Leave some time to see the exhibit on the Great Locomotive Chase, a slapstick adventure involving hand cars, cut wires, and engines traveling in reverse.

ABOVE AND OPPOSITE The Martin Luther King Jr. National Historic Site includes King's tomb and exhibits recalling his leadership in the struggle to end racial segregation in the South. Other stops are his boyhood home and the Ebenezer Baptist Church he served as pastor.

8 *Spreading the Sopchoppy* 6 p.m.

A city where a treasured chef's departure can be front-page news, Atlanta has more than its share of fine restaurants, many of them cavernous, overdesigned colonizations of old industrial buildings. Smaller and friendlier is **Restaurant Eugene** (2277 Peachtree Road; 404-355-0321; restauranteugene.com; $$$), where the staff shares its passions readily and the menu can read like a Southern safari: foie gras on French toast with Sopchoppy brand molasses from Florida; A & J Farms squash blossoms with Anson Mills's grits and Sweetgrass Dairy goat cheese.

9 *Car-Driven Culture* 10 p.m.

The **Starlight Six Drive-In** (2000 Moreland Avenue SE; 404-627-5786; starlightdrivein.com) — "movies and fun since 1949" — has that Southern-culture-on-the-skids charm, retro with a hint of rockabilly. Sometimes used for campy evenings of B-movies and bands (check starlightdrivein.com for the schedule), the rest of the time this is just a straight-up, steamy-windowed cinematic experience in a hummocky parking lot. It's not hard to find a decent movie on the schedule, but bring your own refreshments, as the snack bar is paltry.

SUNDAY

10 *Pancakes and Quiet Neighbors* 10 a.m.

The gruff proprietor of **Ria's Bluebird** (421 Memorial Drive SE; 404-521-3737; riasbluebird.com; $) has the word "hate" tattooed on the nape of her neck. But local residents give her nothing but love, lining up, pleasantly sleep-tousled, on weekend mornings for what some customers say are the world's best pancakes. The light-filled storefront is just right if you feel the need to keep your sun-glasses on in the morning; the floor is made from

wooden wall paneling, creating the illusion of an old barroom. The restaurant is across the street from Atlanta's oldest and loveliest cemetery, **Oakland Cemetery** (248 Oakland Avenue SE; 404-688-2107; oaklandcemetery.com), where Margaret Mitchell, author of *Gone with the Wind*; 25 mayors; and thousands of unidentified Confederate soldiers are buried. In warm weather, guided tours are available on Sunday afternoons.

11 *The King Legacy* 11 a.m.
At the **Martin Luther King Jr. National Historic Site** (450 Auburn Avenue NE; 404-331-6922; nps.gov/malu), you can take a tour of the house where King was born (501 Auburn Avenue NE; reserve

in advance) and, at the visitor center, see his life retraced in photos, print, film, video, and art. If you get an earlier start, you might want to stop by the new Ebenezer Baptist Church, adjacent to the visitor center, for a service. The historic **Old Ebenezer Baptist Church**, where King, his father, and his grandfather preached, is across the street (407 Auburn Avenue NE), no longer used for services but open to view. Inside, in the quiet sanctuary where King's inspiring words once echoed, visitors may find their emotions running high.

OPPOSITE Oakland Cemetery, burial place of 25 Atlanta mayors and Margaret Mitchell, the author of *Gone with the Wind*.

THE BASICS

It is easy to fly nonstop into Hartsfield-Jackson International Airport, a major travel hub.

If you do fly in, rent a car.

Twelve Atlantic Station
361 17th Street NW
404-961-1212
twelvehotels.com
$$$
Full amenities in a bustling Midtown development.

Glenn Hotel
110 Marietta Street N.W.
404-521-2250
glennhotel.com
$$-$$$
Gossamer curtains and a rooftop bar.

Ellis Hotel
176 Peachtree Street N.W.
404-523-5155
ellishotel.com
$$
Functional boutique hotel in a landmark downtown building.

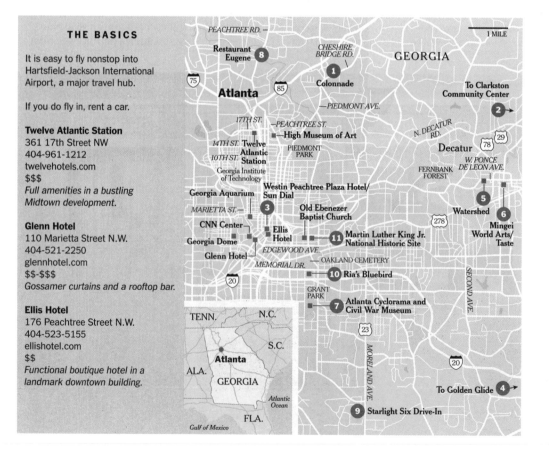

Asheville

Whether it's culture, the great outdoors, or homegrown food and beer, Asheville, North Carolina, takes its pleasures seriously. Playgrounds are equipped with rock-climbing walls. Bumper stickers exhort the locals to buy local. The town is proud of Biltmore, the outsize Vanderbilt mansion, but funds are also being raised for a distinctly more modern kind of museum: tracing the intersection of science and music, and named for Bob Moog, the synthesizer pioneer, who lived in Asheville. All this connoisseurship unfolds, to the benefit of the casual visitor, against the backdrop of the seriously beautiful Blue Ridge Mountains.
— BY SHAILA DEWAN

FRIDAY

1 *Secret (Edible) Garden* 3 p.m.

A small amphitheater, an interactive fountain, and public sculpture adorn the newly redone **Pack Square Park** (packsquarepark.org) at the pink Art Deco-style city hall. But a quick walk away is another, almost secret, park that embodies the scruffy, idealistic side of Asheville: **George Washington Carver Edible Park**. There, the public can graze on apples, chestnuts, and other delectables. To find it, take the outdoor stairway behind Pack's Tavern, go left on Marjorie Street, and cross the pedestrian bridge by the corner of Marjorie and Davidson.

2 *Chai Time* 5 p.m.

Asheville residents love their Indian food, and they are particularly taken with a bright cafe called **Chai Pani** (22 Battery Park Avenue; 828-254-4003; chaipani.net; $) for its fresh, cilantro-strewn takes on Indian street food. For a late-afternoon snack, pop in for a nimbu pani, or salty limeade, and bhel puri, a snack of puffed rice and chickpea noodles in fresh tamarind chutney.

3 *Downtown Drumming* 7 p.m.

There may be 10 onlookers for every drummer at the long-running Friday-night drum circle in triangular **Pritchard Park** (College Street and Patton Avenue) — and there are plenty of drummers. The congas, doumbeks, tambourines, and cowbells provide an ecstatic soundtrack for families, college couples, and dreadlocked nomads. The drum circle is the throbbing heart of downtown, a district of shops, bars, buskers, and street magicians that springs into action as the weekend begins.

4 *Microbrew and a Movie* 9 p.m.

In recent years, Asheville has come to rival Portland, Oregon, as a center for craft beer, and the city has claimed to have more microbreweries per capita — from places like **Green Man Brewery** (greenmanbrewery.com) with its cask-conditioned beers, to the hip **Wedge Brewing Company** (wedgebrewing.com) in the River Arts District. You can try a few on an **Asheville Brews Cruise** tour (brewscruise.com), or linger at the student-friendly **Asheville Pizza and Brewing Company** (675 Merrimon Avenue; 828-254-1281; ashevillebrewing.com), which has a bar, arcade, and cut-rate movie theater. Settle down in front of the large screen with a pint of Rocket Girl or Ninja Porter and a quite respectable pizza (toppings may include Spam, as well as smoked Gouda and artichoke hearts).

SATURDAY

5 *Wood-Fired Breakfast* 9 a.m.

The East-West fusion and wholesome rusticity in Farm and Sparrow's wood-fired pastries

OPPOSITE A class at Black Mountain Yoga. You won't be in Asheville for long before feeling its bohemian spirit.

BELOW Find locally crafted pottery, a western North Carolina specialty, at Curve Studios in the River Arts District.

seem to sum up Asheville. The croissants stuffed with kimchi and an open-faced pear, Gorgonzola, and bee pollen confection are made at the bakery (farmandsparrow.com) in nearby Candler, N.C., and are available at some of Asheville's tailgate markets, a kind of hyper-local version of a farmers' market. The **North Asheville Tailgate Market** (828-712-4644; northashevilletailgatemarket.org), held in a parking lot on the campus of the University of North Carolina at Asheville, is where you'll also find locally made kombucha from Buchi, trout dip from the Sunburst Trout Company, and fresh goat cheese with lavender from Three Graces Dairy.

6 *Mountain Stretch* 10:30 a.m.

Like any bohemian resort worth its coarse-ground Himalayan salt, Asheville has its share of healing arts. Find spa treatments, colonics, and "affordable acupuncture" at the **Thrifty Taoist** in the town of Black Mountain (106 Black Mountain Avenue; 828-713-9185; thriftytaoist.com), about 15 minutes from downtown. **Black Mountain Yoga** offers one-on-one yoga therapy sessions with Martia Rachman and her husband, Brad, a naturopath (120 Broadway Street, Black Mountain; 828-669-2939; blackmountainyoga.com). While you perform stretches and poses, one of the Rachmans will identify problem areas and massage and manipulate stubborn muscles. An hour later, a looser, more relaxed you will emerge from their clutches.

7 *Artists' Utopia* Noon

Short-lived but enormously influential, **Black Mountain College** (blackmountaincollege.org) was evidence of Asheville's pull on the unconventionally creative. John Cage, Merce Cunningham, Buckminster Fuller, and Josef Albers were among the teachers at this oft-re-examined intellectual utopia that closed, after a quarter-century, in the late 1950s. The campus at Lake Eden (375 Lake Eden Road, Black Mountain) is now a Christian boys' camp, but when it is not in session you can still inspect the Bauhaus-inspired main campus building and fading murals by Jean

Charlot. Twice a year, the **Lake Eden Arts Festival** (828-686-8742; theleaf.org) unfolds there.

8 *Robot vs. Mermaid* 2 p.m.

Western North Carolina is known for pottery, and you can find some of the artists themselves at work at **Curve Studios** in the River Arts District (6, 9, and 12 Riverside Drive; 828-388-3526; curvestudiosnc.com). At the showroom-cum-studios, you might find robot vases by Patty Bilbro ($165), a mermaid figurine by Fran Welch ($35), or sophisticated tableware by Akira Satake and Maria Andrade Troya.

9 *Old-Time Architecture* 3 p.m.

On the Obamas' Asheville vacation in 2010, they joined a long line of presidents and celebrities who have stayed at the **Grove Park Inn** (290 Macon Avenue; 800-438-5800; groveparkinn.com), a giant pile of rocks topped by a red roof that looks like melting snow. The inn retains a Craftsman-era grace, despite some remodeling involving a good deal of wood paneling. Take in the splendor of the Great Hall—and a Great Hall Bloody, the definitive bloody mary—accompanied by the local bands that play mostly old-time, Americana, and bluegrass music on Saturday afternoons.

10 *Toast to Literature* 5 p.m.

The **Battery Park Book Exchange and Champagne Bar** (Grove Arcade, 1 Page Avenue; 828-252-0020; batteryparkbookexchange.com) is not a place to find shabby paperbacks. Instead, think never-read leather-bound volumes of Dickens ($435 for a set), an edition of *The Catcher in the Rye* with the carousel horse cover ($200), acres of gardening and art hardbacks, and a glass of fizzy Heidsieck & Co. Monopole ($15). The Mission-style sofas and leather armchairs in book-lined alcoves bring the cozy nook idea to a new level.

11 *Gastro-Dive* 8 p.m.

What are truffles, steak tartare, and imported oysters doing in a cinderblock dive bar amid the cool haunts of West Asheville? One bite of dinner at the **Admiral** (400 Haywood Road; 828-252-2541; theadmiralnc.com) and such questions subside into flavor combinations like balsamic pears with honey cap mushrooms or foie gras with Nutella. When new owners bought the old B&D Bar, renamed it, and installed a gastropub with an ever-changing menu, the Admiral became Asheville's hottest restaurant; reservations recommended. Late on Saturday nights, the tables are cleared away for a crowded and sweaty dance party.

SUNDAY

12 *Treetop Zip* 9 a.m.

Leaf peeping is a serious sport in Asheville — hence the weekly "fall color report" from the local visitor's bureau (exploreasheville.com). Experience the local treetops, whatever the season, from a

whole new angle on the three-and-a-half-hour zipline course at **Navitat Canopy Adventures**, about 20 minutes north of town (242 Poverty Branch Road, Barnardsville; 828-626-3700; navitat.com). Wearing a hard hat, you'll be strapped in and hooked up with a series of reassuring clicks for each of the 10 zips, the longest at 1,100 feet. They take you from chestnut oaks to tulip poplars, soaring over valleys with a bird's-eye view that will remind you, once again, of the Blue Ridge bedrock of Asheville's eternal appeal.

OPPOSITE The Friday drum circle at Pritchard Park draws families, college couples, and dreadlocked nomads.

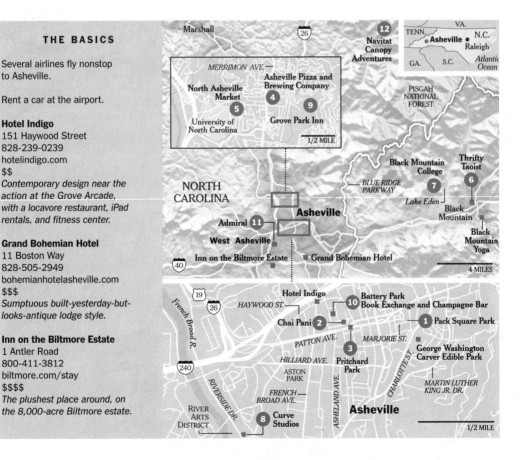

THE BASICS

Several airlines fly nonstop to Asheville.

Rent a car at the airport.

Hotel Indigo
151 Haywood Street
828-239-0239
hotelindigo.com
$$
Contemporary design near the action at the Grove Arcade, with a locavore restaurant, iPad rentals, and fitness center.

Grand Bohemian Hotel
11 Boston Way
828-505-2949
bohemianhotelasheville.com
$$$
Sumptuous built-yesterday-but-looks-antique lodge style.

Inn on the Biltmore Estate
1 Antler Road
800-411-3812
biltmore.com/stay
$$$$
The plushest place around, on the 8,000-acre Biltmore estate.

Gatlinburg

Gatlinburg, Tennessee, the gateway town to Great Smoky Mountains National Park, has a string of garish tourist traps on its congested main street, but no amount of over-the-top hucksterism can spoil its setting, nudged up against the misty blue peaks of the Smokies. The park is spectacular all year, with deep-green canopies in summer, red and gold vistas in fall, and blankets of white in winter. Perhaps the best time to visit is spring, when orchids and violets bloom in its half-million acres of rolling hills, whitewater tumbles on the rivers, festivals spill into the streets of Gatlinburg, and bluegrass twangs in the air.
— BY SARAH TUFF

FRIDAY

1 *United Artists* 3:30 p.m.

One of the greatest achievements by any sorority might be the 1912 founding of the Settlement School by the Pi Beta Phi sisters, who aimed to educate the Appalachian poor. Eventually, it became the **Arrowmont School of Arts and Crafts** (556 Parkway; 865-436-5860; arrowmont.org), a funky, airy studio and gallery in downtown Gatlinburg. (Or, as one online travel forum user wrote, an oasis in a sea of fudge.) It's free and open — with occasional workshops and an adjacent craft shop — until 4:30 p.m. Peer in on artists at work from the catwalk that runs above separate studios, or admire oil paintings, woodwork, and delicate sterling-silver sculptures in the three galleries.

2 *Tourists Trapped* 5 p.m.

Many tourists who travel to Gatlinburg don't know about Great Smoky Mountains National Park. Shocking — but then again there do seem to be quite a lot of distractions along the Parkway, the main drag that leads through town to the park. The **Space Needle** (115 Historic Nature Trail; 865-436-4629; gatlinburgspaceneedle.com) is a 1970 landmark with an elevator that whisks, well, works its way

OPPOSITE Laurel Creek near Cades Cove in Great Smoky Mountains National Park.

RIGHT The Smoky Mountain Trout House, one place in town to eat the favorite local fish.

342 feet up for an open-air, 360-degree view. At **Ripley's Believe It or Not! Museum** (800 Parkway; 865-436-5096; gatlinburg.ripleys.com), you can gawk at attractions like a 6,600-foot gum wrapper chain, shrunken heads, and locusts preserved from an 1860 plague. There's also a haunted house that might actually spook you and, down the road, an aquarium with a walk-through shark lagoon. But nothing as scary as the museum's sushi lint art and 5.5-pound pig hairball.

3 *Tequila Wish, Tortilla Dream* 7:30 p.m.

Hungry? After Ripley's, you're probably not in the mood for sushi — or anything that has to do with a pig. But your appetite will quickly return after a pitcher or two of margaritas on the outdoor deck at **No Way Jose's Cantina** (555 Parkway; 865-430-5673; nowayjosescantina.com; $), a Tex-Mex joint overlooking the Little Pigeon River. Try the deep fried ice cream, adorned with cinnamon, honey, chocolate, and whipped cream. Before you get to that, go for the fajitas. But nothing too spicy — you're hiking tomorrow morning, and servicios are scarce to nonexistent along those Great Smoky trails.

SATURDAY

4 *Stacked in Your Favor* 7 a.m.

If you're staying along the Little Pigeon River, you might rise to the sight of an angler trying to

reel in a trout. An easier way to find breakfast is at one of Gatlinburg's pancake parlors, whose choices might leave you reeling yourself. The **Pancake Pantry** (628 Parkway; 865-436-4724; pancakepantry.com; $), which says it became Tennessee's first pancake house in 1960, now flips 24 varieties, including apricot lemon and Peach Delight. The Pantry will also pack you an inexpensive lunch for the park.

5 *Chasing Waterfalls* 8 a.m.

Drop the pancake fork. Slowly back away from any nearby candy shop. There are more than 800 miles of hiking trails in **Great Smoky Mountains National Park** (nps.gov/grsm) and nearly as many waterfalls. You will have most of the footpaths and falling water all to yourself, perhaps shared with a few of the 31 species of salamanders that slither through the Smokies, an area known for the rich diversity of its critters. **Ramsey Cascades** (off Route 321, past the Greenbrier entrance and ranger station) is a rugged eight-mile round-trip hike that gains about 2,140 feet in altitude. It takes you through the Smokies' largest chunk of old-growth forest — cherry, hemlock, and tulip trees — before arriving at the 90-foot falls and its cooling spray. Another path in the Smokies is the Appalachian Trail; when the through-hikers walking it from Georgia to Maine get to Gatlinburg, they are 200 miles, or about 9 percent, of the way into the trip.

6 *Rapid Transit* 3 p.m.

When Daniel Jennette, a river-rafting guide with **Smoky Mountain Outdoors** (453 Brookside Village Way; 800-771-7238; smokymountainrafting.com), chose Lost Guide as the name for one of the 70 rapids on a 6.5-mile stretch of the upper Big Pigeon River,

he wasn't joking. The Class IV is where most new guides — and you, the rookie rafter — tumble into the drink during a two-hour trip. Your best shot at staying dry (or at least dryish) is to keep paddling, maintain your center of gravity, and stay tough. Be ready for the first Class IV, 30 seconds into the trip, and for the more placid After Shave and Bombs Lake sections, where you can finally kick back for a couple of minutes. For a lazier float, rent inner tubes from Smoky Mountain and ply the Little River, or consider the gentle lower Big Pigeon, where even young children are allowed to go rafting.

7 *Bottoms Up* 6:30 p.m.

The brew master Marty Velas, who helped open the **Smoky Mountain Brewery** (1004 Parkway; 865-436-4200; coppercellar.com) in 1996, knows a thing or two about beer. He has collected some 6,000 bottles, half of which are lined along the exposed beams upstairs in this brewery pub. Try the Mountain Light or, should you need more recovery from the rafting, the more potent Black Bear Ale.

8 *Trout and About* 8 p.m.

Remember that trout that got away, around breakfast time today? Look for its cousin, boned and pan-fried, next door to the Smoky Mountain Brewery at the **Park Grill** (1110 Parkway; 865-436-2300; parkgrillgatlinburg.com; $$). Or satisfy your inner carnivore, if you must, with one of the hefty steaks. Then it's back to the brewery, where the band will start playing around 9:30.

ABOVE Black Bear Ale at the Smoky Mountain Brewery, a place to recover after a day of exploring. Look for hikers who have detoured into town from the Appalachian Trail.

SUNDAY

9 *Tennessee Shangri-La* 8 a.m.

About 30 miles into Great Smoky Mountains National Park from Gatlinburg, **Cades Cove** is a cluster of 19th-century cabins, mills, and churches in a wide green valley, now left to the deer, otter, bears, and wild turkeys. At midday, cars clog the 11-mile loop around the cove, but if you get an early start, you can avoid the crush and enjoy the area on a bicycle (nps.gov/grsm/planyourvisit/biking.htm). Things are even better on summer Wednesday and Saturday mornings, when the area is open only to hikers and cyclists until 10 a.m. You can rent bikes at the **Cades Cove Campground Store**

(865-448-9034; cadescove.net). Or hop on a horse at the nearby **Cades Cove Riding Stable** (423-448-6286; cadescovestables.com).

10 *Justly Deserved* Noon

Be sure you don't leave Gatlinburg without stopping by **Desserts & More**, at Sweetpea's Cafe & Antique Lounge (458 Parkway; 865-277-7711; dessertsandmore.com). This is home cooking, from thick chicken-salad sandwiches to fluffy coconut pie and creamy chocolate-chip cheesecake, all made from scratch. Enjoy them with homemade lemonade and flavored iced teas. Slices or entire pies and cakes are available to go — though chances are they won't make it very far.

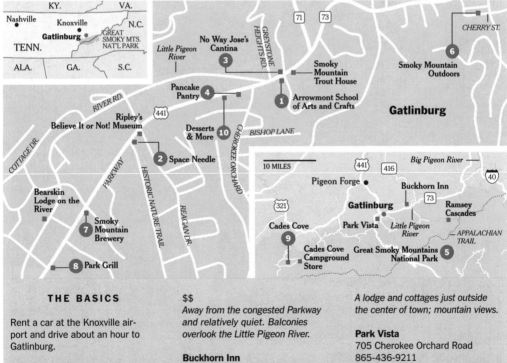

THE BASICS

Rent a car at the Knoxville airport and drive about an hour to Gatlinburg.

Bearskin Lodge on the River
840 River Road
865-430-4330
thebearskinlodge.com

$$
Away from the congested Parkway and relatively quiet. Balconies overlook the Little Pigeon River.

Buckhorn Inn
2140 Tudor Mountain Road
865-436-4668
buckhorninn.com
$$-$$$

A lodge and cottages just outside the center of town; mountain views.

Park Vista
705 Cherokee Orchard Road
865-436-9211
parkvista.com
$$
Recently renovated Doubletree property on a mountaintop site.

Knoxville

Knoxville, Tennessee, is often called "the couch" by the people who live there. It is a place too unassuming to shout about but too comfortable to leave. The city, the third largest in Tennessee behind Nashville and Memphis, is also referred to as Knoxpatch, Knoxvegas, and for those prone to irony and finger pistols, K-town, baby. The truth is, Knoxville, a college town cheerfully ensconced in the foothills of the Great Smoky Mountains and banked against the Tennessee River, has an intrinsically lazy, soulful air about it. The geography is soft, green, and rolling. The climate is gentle, breezy, and bright. Locals tend to be not just friendly — a given in most Southern towns — but chilled out, too. This is not the Old South of magnolias and seersucker so much as a modern Appalachia of roots music, locavore food, folk art, and hillbilly pride. Or, as yet another city moniker aptly puts it, "Austin without the hype." — BY ALLISON GLOCK

FRIDAY

1 *Cultivated Bluegrass* Noon

Knoxville is known for its music — Dolly Parton was discovered here, Hank Williams stopped here

OPPOSITE Sequoyah Hills Park has 87 acres of land with trails for walking, running, and biking, as well as free boat access to the Tennessee River.

BELOW The Sunsphere was built for a 1982 world's fair.

on his last road trip, and most locals know their way around a banjo. The listener-supported station **WDVX-FM**, multiple winner of the national title Bluegrass Station of the Year, hosts the Monday-through-Saturday *Blue Plate Special* show, offering free live music from noon to 1 p.m. (301 South Gay Street; 865-544-1029; wdvx.com). Guests include everyone from Béla Fleck and Ricky Skaggs to the Gypsy jazz band Ameranouche and homegrown Appalachian talent. Bring a bag lunch or pick up an ice-cold cola and some snacks from the old-fashioned mercantile **Mast General Store** (402 South Gay Street; 865-546-1336; mastgeneralstore.com) and take a seat for some down-home music in an unusually intimate setting.

2 *Art for All Y'all* 2 p.m.

Part gallery, part stationery shop, all handmade cool, **Yee-Haw Industries** (413 South Gay Street; 865-522-1812; yeehawindustries.com) is a great spot to idle for an hour or two, soaking up the walls and ceilings blanketed with one-of-a-kind letterpress posters, bags, shirts, calendars, and fine art prints. Stop in and chat with the owner-artists Julie Belcher and Kevin Bradley, who, if you're lucky, will take you upstairs to show you their latest projects, most painstakingly created from carved woodblock, then letterpressed using vintage machinery. The results are distinctive, beautiful, and evocative of the past. If nothing else, pick up some cards. The sets, hand printed on 100 percent recycled stock, are unlike anything you're likely to find at Hallmark.

3 *Meats and Sweets* 5 p.m.

Litton's (2803 Essary Road; 865-687-8788; littonburgers.com; $) is a bit off the beaten path, which doesn't keep it from being standing room only virtually every lunch and dinner. Started in a small back room, the diner-style restaurant, meat market, and bakery has sprawled to fill a warehouse's worth of space. Known for its burgers and desserts, Litton's is not the place to come if cholesterol is a preoccupation. Go for the Thunder Road burger (pimento cheese, sautéed onions, and jalapeño with fries) and a slice of red velvet cake. Lines are long, but pews are available while you wait. Just be sure to sign in on the chalkboard.

SATURDAY

4 *Green Acres* 8 a.m.

Jog, walk, bike, or paddle at **Sequoyah Hills Park** (1400 Cherokee Boulevard; ci.knoxville.tn.us/parks/sequoyah.asp), an 87-acre sprawl of green lawns, flowering trees, dog paths, and picnic spots on the Tennessee River. Water access is easy, as is parking. For a longer hike, the **Ijams Nature Center** (2915 Island Home Avenue; 865-577-4717; ijams.org), a 160-acre park and wildlife sanctuary, is a 10-minute drive from downtown.

5 *Pioneer Spirit* 11 a.m.

Twenty minutes outside Knoxville will take you to the **Museum of Appalachia** (2819 Andersonville Highway, Clinton; 865-494-7680; museumofappalachia.org). Born of the historian John Rice Irwin's love for the mountain people of Tennessee, the museum encompasses truckloads of Appalachian pioneer artifacts and folk art as well as actual cabins, churches, and outbuildings that were carefully moved from their original locations and reassembled on its expansive grounds. Live music can be heard almost every day thanks to the Porch Musicians Project, Irwin's effort to expose all guests to "authentic old-time music" and preserve America's aural history. Lunch is available in the cafe. Order the fresh-fried pinto beans and cornbread.

6 *Let Them Eat Cupcakes* 4 p.m.

Cupcake mania has swept the nation. But nowhere is it more deserved than at **MagPies** (846 North Central Street; 865-673-0471; magpiescakes.com), a place whose motto is "all butter all the time." The baker, proprietress, and adequate accordion player Peggy Hambright specializes in "super deluxe flavors" that change every month. (Examples: Chocolate Guinness Stout, Key lime pie, and blackberry buttermilk.) A dozen minis or a six-pack of regulars, the usual units of purchase, may seem like a lot to buy at once, but don't plan on any leftovers.

7 *Say Tomato* 7 p.m.

The nexus for all things hip and happening in town, the vegan-friendly **Tomato Head** (12 Market Square; 865-637-4067; thetomatohead.com; $$), is the place to go for epicurean pizza and unparalleled people watching. The founder, chef, and local foodie icon Mahasti Vafaie makes everything you eat there, including the breads, buns, and salad dressings. Order the No. 8 (pesto-based pizza with Roma tomato and roasted portobello), the Greek salad (heavy on the kalamata olives), and a glass of wine. Sit outside

if you can, where your table overlooks the whole of Market Square — a cheek-by-jowl assortment of cafes, boutiques, galleries, and pubs all with a bustling shared common area.

8 *Square Deal* 8:30 p.m.

Market Square restaurants have outdoor seating, and most evenings find amateur pickers and singers performing in the square, lending the whole space the feeling of a giant impromptu party. Stores worth some après dinner window shopping include **Reruns Consignment Boutique** (2 Market Square; 865-525-9525; rerunsboutique.com) for bargain-priced designer finds and **Bliss** (24 Market Square; 865-329-8868; shopinbliss.com), an everything-but-the-kitchen-sink gift emporium offering apparel, furniture, frames, and flatware.

ABOVE Poster making at Yee-Haw Industries.

BELOW A mural of a London Street in the Crown & Goose English-style pub, where brunch can include Stilton cheese.

9 *Ale Power* 10 p.m.

Amid the Market Square madness sits the **Preservation Pub** (28 Market Square; 865-524-2224; preservationpub.com), a narrow slip of a bar that manages to squeeze quite a few folks and even more beer choices into its cozy confines. There are 20-plus strong ale selections alone (try the Stone Arrogant Bastard or the Orkney Skull Splitter) but know that the bartenders keep an eye on the number of strong ales you down, so as to avoid chaos spilling onto the square — unless it is live music night. Then all bets are off.

SUNDAY

10 *English Eaten Here* 11 a.m.

The Crown & Goose gastropub (123 South Central Street; 865-524-2100; thecrownandgoose.com; $$)

serves a hearty brunch along with whatever soccer match happens to be on TV that day. Sidle up to the huge 19th-century-style bar and sample the eggs Benedict with fried green tomatoes or the Belgian waffles dipped in cider batter and loaded with sweet cream cheese, maple syrup, and fresh fruit. Traditional English fare is also on offer, from a cheese board that includes Stilton to the requisite fish and chips.

11 *Heights and Hoops* 3 p.m.

Before you leave, take the elevator to the top of the **Sunsphere** (810 Clinch Avenue), an architectural leftover from the 1982 World's Fair and a parody victim of *The Simpsons*. The Sunsphere, a 600-ton,

266-foot steel truss topped with a 74-foot gold ball, looks like a Titleist on steroids but offers the best views of the city and the mountains just beyond. The **Women's Basketball Hall of Fame** (700 Hall of Fame Drive; 865-633-9000; wbhof.com) is the home of the world's largest basketball — 30 feet tall, 10 tons, no Sunsphere, but still — and myriad artifacts of early women's basketball from throughout the world, including an original 1901 rulebook. Of course, tributes to Pat Summit, the coach of the hometown University of Tennessee Lady Vols, who has the most victories in Division 1 basketball history (well over 1,000 and counting), rightfully abound.

ABOVE One of the preserved historic buildings moved to the grounds of the Museum of Appalachia, a treasure trove of pioneer artifacts and folk art.

OPPOSITE The exterior of the Crown & Goose.

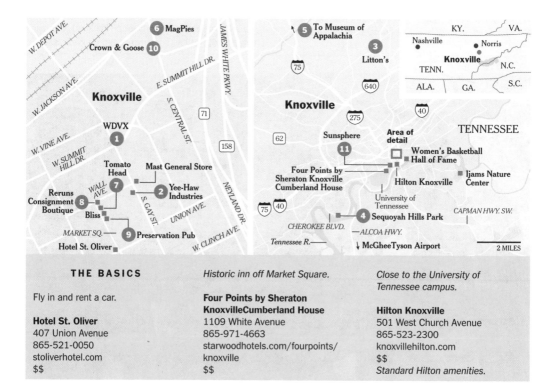

THE BASICS

Fly in and rent a car.

Hotel St. Oliver
407 Union Avenue
865-521-0050
stoliverhotel.com
$$

Historic inn off Market Square.

Four Points by Sheraton KnoxvilleCumberland House
1109 White Avenue
865-971-4663
starwoodhotels.com/fourpoints/knoxville
$$

Close to the University of Tennessee campus.

Hilton Knoxville
501 West Church Avenue
865-523-2300
knoxvillehilton.com
$$
Standard Hilton amenities.

Lexington

Miles of low fences line the winding, two-lane roads of the Bluegrass Country around Lexington, Kentucky, and enclose its rolling green horse farms, where magnificent thoroughbreds rest near pristinely painted barns. Now and again, the fences break for a leafy lane leading to an age-old bourbon distillery with doors open for a tour and a tipple. Then they lead away to a quaint 19th-century town, a quintessential country inn, or a serene Shaker village. These magical fences, made of wood or of stones stacked long ago by slaves and Scots-Irish settlers, take you back in time and away in space. But you'll be brought back soon enough by Kentucky's modern hosts serving up Southern charm and distinctly American food and drink. — BY TAYLOR HOLLIDAY

FRIDAY

1 *Horse Fixation* 1:45 p.m.

Lexington, a leisurely university city with preserved antebellum houses, calls itself the horse capital of the world. On thousands of acres of nearby farms, pampered horses graze on the local bluegrass, so called because it blooms a purplish blue. Dip into the horse world at **Kentucky Horse Park** (4089 Iron Works Parkway, Lexington; 859-233-4303; kyhorsepark.com). It may seem at first like merely a giant horsy theme park, but the horse trailers in the parking lot attest to its importance for competitions as well. There are displays on the history of the horse, paeans to winners like Man o' War and Cigar, and a Parade of Breeds (catch it at 2 p.m.). Horse shows and races are frequent — you might catch a steeplechase. And in June, musicians arrive from far and wide for a festival of bluegrass music.

2 *Chefs of the Country* 7 p.m.

Northwest of Lexington, Route 62 cuts a path through lush countryside to charming little Midway, a railroad town of about 1,600 people where trains still run right down the middle of the main street. A gem

of a restaurant, the **Holly Hill Inn** (426 North Winter Street, Midway; 859-846-4732; hollyhillinn.com; $$$), awaits you down a nearby lane, in a house dating to 1839. Ouita Michel, the chef, and her husband, Chris, the sommelier, both graduates of the Culinary Institute of America, serve a four-course prix fixe dinner. Choices on the changing menus have included spoonbread souffle, pork roast with figs and dates, and tile fish with Kentucky red rice.

SATURDAY

3 *Brake for Bourbon* 10 a.m.

The land around Lexington grows more than thoroughbreds. West of the city, you're in bourbon country. Several distillers have banded together to create what they call the Bourbon Trail, so spend a day learning why their product is such a source of Kentucky pride. Stop first in Versailles (pronounce it "ver-SALES"), where the stately limestone **Woodford Reserve** (7855 McCracken Pike; 859-879-1812; woodfordreserve.com) is nestled deep among farms with cupola-topped stables and miles of black-painted board fences. The only product made here is the small-batch Woodford Reserve, but visitors come by the thousands, and you'll see the entire bourbon-making process from mash to bottle. Inhale the smells of whiskey and old wood, and sip a sample.

OPPOSITE White rail fences mark the rolling green fields of a horse farm in Kentucky Bluegrass Country.

RIGHT Woodford Reserve, one of the Kentucky bourbon distilleries where a tour is capped with a sip of the whiskey.

4 *Whiskey Saga* Noon

Bardstown, a city of about 10,000 in the heart of bourbon territory, honors its debt to spirits at the **Oscar Getz Museum of Whiskey History** (114 North Fifth Street; 502-348-2999; whiskeymuseum.com). In the 1790s, Scotch-Irish distillers fleeing George Washington's whiskey tax and the quelling of the subsequent Whiskey Rebellion landed in an area of Virginia then called Bourbon County, which now covers several counties of northeastern Kentucky. They found perfect conditions for their trade, partly because of a layer of limestone that filters iron from the local water, and bourbon whiskey was born. In the museum, examine local artifacts including authentic moonshine stills.

5 *Vary the Stimuli* 1 p.m.

Make a temporary switch from booze to caffeine at **Java Joint** (126 North 3rd Street, Bardstown; 502-350-0883; thejavajoint.homestead.com; $), where you can grab a quick lunch of sandwiches, soup, or salad along with the signature cup of flavorful coffee.

6 *Dip Your Own* 2 p.m.

Meander about 15 miles south on Route 49 to tiny Loretto and enter the red-shuttered, brown-clapboard buildings of **Maker's Mark** (3350 Burks Springs Road; 270-865-2099). The oldest bourbon distillery in the country, dating to 1805, it is well schooled in the rules

of bourbon: the mash must be at least 51 percent corn, barrels for aging must be new and made of charred white oak, alcohol must be at prescribed strengths in the years-long process of transforming grain into whiskey. The tour here shows you the cooker, mash fermentation, the still, aging rackhouses, and hand-bottling. You can dip a finger into a vat of bubbling, fermenting mash to get a taste (like sweetened cereal gone sour), and they'll even let you hand-dip your own souvenir bottle in the trademark red wax.

7 *Jim Beam's Place* 4 p.m.

Drive back north to Bardstown and take Route 245 west to Clermont, the home of **Jim Beam** (149 Happy Hollow Road; 502-543-9877; jimbeam.com), the biggest of the bourbon distillers. Jim Beam doesn't have an extensive tour, but you'll get a good tasting. And from the porch of the Beam family's whitewashed mansion on the hill, you have a perfect view of the vapor-spewing, multibuilding factory, which has turned out millions of bottles of bourbon.

8 *Not a Colonel in Sight* 6 p.m.

For real Kentucky skillet-fried chicken, take a table at **Kurtz** (418 East Stephen Foster Avenue, Bardstown; 502-348-8964; bardstownparkview.com/dining.htm; $$), which has been satisfying hungry Kentuckians for 70 years. The chicken is superb and the fixings are traditional—mashed potatoes,

cornbread, green beans with Kentucky ham. For dessert, ask for the biscuit pudding with bourbon sauce.

9 *Bourbons by the Dozen* 8 p.m.

When you're finished with the day's driving and ready to relax, sample the atmosphere and the libations at a bourbon bar, where knowledgeable bartenders serve Kentucky's favorite drink in dozens of varieties. In Bardstown, there's a classic of the genre at **Old Talbott Tavern** (107 West Stephen Foster Avenue; 502-348-3494; talbotts.com). In Lexington, try **Bluegrass Tavern** (115 Cheapside, Lexington; 859-389-6664) or the **Horse and Barrel Pub** at deSha's Restaurant and Bar (101 North Broadway; 859-259-3771; tavernrestaurantgroup.com).

SUNDAY

10 *Thoroughbreds at Home* 9 a.m.

Taking tourists to the horse farms is a Lexington specialty—the local convention and visitors bureau publishes a list of tour companies and private guides (visitlex.com/idea/horse-farms.php). One good choice is a trip with the women of **Horse Farm Tours** (859-268-2906; horsefarmtours.com), who point out historical buildings in downtown Lexington on the way to a sampling of farms. If decadently luxurious stables and a 10-bedroom mansion at one farm are a reminder that thoroughbreds are a rich person's

hobby, the wholesome young broodmare manager at the next farm, attending to the mares and their wobbly, week-old foals, is proof of how intense the horse-and-human relationship can be. At the stud farm, it's all about bloodlines and breeding techniques. You'll also be whisked to the best seats in the ivy-covered

OPPOSITE Oak barrels at Woodford Reserve. On the tour, you'll see the bourbon-making process from mash to bottle.

TOP Green countryside near Loretto, on one of the winding side roads to explore near Lexington.

ABOVE Whiskey makers migrated to this part of Kentucky, then known as Bourbon County, Virginia, around 1800. Some of their tools are displayed at Maker's Mark distillery.

limestone viewing stand at Keeneland, Lexington's renowned race track — to see, perhaps, some horses in training.

11 *Plain Cooking* 1 p.m.

Drive south from Lexington on Route 68, through gently undulating hills and higher forested bluffs, to **Shaker Village of Pleasant Hill** (3501 Lexington Road, Harrodsburg; 859-734-5411; shakervillageky.org), a preserved home of the plain-living 19th-century Shaker sect. It feels remarkably like the real deal; the most beautiful of its 34 remaining buildings needed only light restoration to return them to the middle 1800s, when the community was at its peak. (Shakerism embraced celibacy and eventually died out.) Have dinner in the spare and lovely Trustees' Office Dining Room restaurant (call for reservations), which cooks with heirloom vegetables from its own garden, and tour the quiet grounds.

ABOVE Maker's Mark, in Loretto, finishes off its bourbon bottles with signature red wax.

OPPOSITE Inside a storage warehouse at the Jim Beam distillery in Clermont.

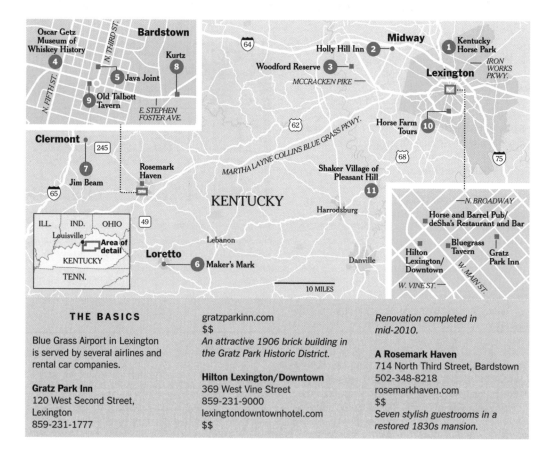

THE BASICS

Blue Grass Airport in Lexington is served by several airlines and rental car companies.

Gratz Park Inn
120 West Second Street, Lexington
859-231-1777

gratzparkinn.com
$$
An attractive 1906 brick building in the Gratz Park Historic District.

Hilton Lexington/Downtown
369 West Vine Street
859-231-9000
lexingtondowntownhotel.com
$$

Renovation completed in mid-2010.

A Rosemark Haven
714 North Third Street, Bardstown
502-348-8218
rosemarkhaven.com
$$
Seven stylish guestrooms in a restored 1830s mansion.

Louisville

Every May, Louisville, Kentucky, bolts into the public eye for 120 seconds — the time it takes to run the Kentucky Derby. But there is more to this courtly city on the Ohio River than the Derby. The last decade has seen a cultural and civic blooming, with new galleries, restaurants, and performance spaces taking their place alongside the city's already robust roster of seductions. Entire neighborhoods — Butchertown, for instance, and East Market — have been reimagined as engines of cultural and culinary expression. Regardless of the changes, Derby City retains its easy charm — a glass of fine bourbon and good conversation aren't hard to find. And for the record, it's pronounced "LOU-uh-vull."
— BY MICHAEL WASHBURN

FRIDAY

1 *Getting Acquainted* 6 p.m.

More than 45 different watering holes line the roughly two miles of the Bardstown Road-Baxter Avenue corridor, from elegant restaurants to sticky-floored dives. Sandwiched among them are cafes, galleries specializing in regional ceramics and woodwork, and shops selling vintage clothing and jewelry, musical instruments, and Louisville-themed curiosities. A welcome addition is the **Holy Grale** (1034 Bardstown Road; 502-459-9939; holygralelouisville.com). Recently opened in a century-old church, this dark, snug tavern with a polished bar running its length offers a selection of fine beers, including 20 rare drafts like the unpasteurized Aecht Schlenkerla Rauchbier Urbock, a dark beer that is surprisingly light despite its smoky, chocolate flavor. The chorizo tacos make a fiery complement.

2 *Bootleggers and Grits* 8:30 p.m.

Jack Fry's (1007 Bardstown Road; 502-452-9244; jackfrys.com; $$$) opened in 1933 as a haven for bootleggers and bookies and has remained a popular dining spot, with its classic Old South atmosphere and original décor. A collection of 1930s-era photographs — including shots of the 1937 flood that devastated

downtown Louisville and prompted development in the eastern, now more affluent, sections of town — adorns the walls, and a discreet jazz trio performs in the corner. These days the restaurant focuses on subtle reinventions of Southern staples: shrimp and grits with red-eye gravy and country ham, for example, or lamb chops in a rosemary natural jus with shiitakes and thyme.

3 *Night Music* 10:30 p.m.

From Will Oldham and Slint to My Morning Jacket, Louisville performers have sent their music echoing around the world. Even if you're not lucky enough to catch Oldham or MMJ in one of their local appearances, with other talent — like Wax Fang, Cheyenne Mize, Seluah, and Joe Manning — you can always find something to spirit you away. **Zanzabar** (2100 South Preston Street; 502-635-9227; zanzabarlouisville.com) offers cheap whiskey for you to sip at its horseshoe-shaped bar while you catch one of the city's (or country's) comers on its intimate stage. Closing time here — and almost everywhere in Louisville — is 4 a.m.

SATURDAY

4 *Art and Comfort Food* 9 a.m.

The East Market District, dubbed NuLu (new Louisville) is perhaps the best of the city's revitalization projects, offering antiques stores and shiny new galleries. The **Zephyr Gallery** (610 East Market Street; 502-585-5646; zephyrgallery.org) and **Swanson Reed Contemporary** (638 East Market Street; 502-589-5466; swansonreedgallery.com) display paintings, videos, and installation work from

OPPOSITE On the track at the Kentucky Derby.

RIGHT The Moonshine Breakfast at Hillbilly Tea.

regional and national artists. Before exploring too far, visit the new **Hillbilly Tea** (120 South First Street; 502-587-7350; hillbillytea.com; $$) for the Moonshine Breakfast: a grilled pork chop with bourbon and sage, herb scrambled eggs, and potatoes. The gettin's good, and the locals know it, so be patient.

5 *Float Like a Butterfly* 11 a.m.

Louisville's greatest son is the greatest: Muhammad Ali. The **Muhammad Ali Center** (144 North Sixth Street; 502-584-9254; alicenter.org) celebrates his singular talent as a fighter and his post-retirement humanitarian efforts, but the curators pulled no punches with the history. Sure, you can try the speed bag, but not before you're immersed in multimedia presentations that contextualize Ali's career within the civil rights struggle. The Ali Center is part of **Museum Row** (museumrowonmain.com), an eclectic confederation of museums and galleries devoted to science, blown glass art, Louisville Slugger baseball bats, historical artifacts (including armor worn by English knights), and more.

6 *Riders Up!* 1:30 p.m.

Churchill Downs (700 Central Avenue; 502-636-4400; churchilldowns.com) demands a visit even if you're not here for the Derby — especially if you're not here for the Derby. During other races in the spring meet, which runs for several months,

a spot on Millionaire's Row costing Diddy and his ilk $68,000 on Derby Day will set you back only $20 when you walk among the mortals; don't worry, the ponies charge just as hard. Adjacent to the Downs, the **Kentucky Derby Museum** (704 Central Avenue; 502-637-7097; derbymuseum.org), open all year, offers an overview of the Run for the Roses and hosts several track tours, including one of the "backside," home to 1,400 thoroughbreds during racing season. After leaving the Downs, visit **Wagner's Pharmacy** (3113 South

ABOVE Reliving the Derby at the Kentucky Derby Museum.

BELOW Churchill Downs, active on more than Derby Day.

OPPOSITE Holy Grale, a stop on the bar strip.

Fourth Street; 502-375-3800; wagnerspharmacy.com), fabled hangout of grooms, jockeys, and sportswriters. Barely changed since 1922, Wagner's lunch counter displays fading photos of legends—two- and four-legged—from Derby history.

7 *Whiskey Row* 6 p.m.

Doc Crows (127 West Main Street; 502-587-1626; doccrows.com; $$) occupies the former Bonnie Bros. distillery, one of Louisville's collection of cast-iron-facade buildings in an area called Whiskey Row. Take a seat in the back room of this 1880s-era gem and enjoy oysters on the half shell with bourbon mignonette or Carolina-style pulled pork. Brett Davis, an owner, one of 112 master sommeliers in the country, prowls about most nights. Ask Brett to select which of the 64 bourbons will go best with your meal.

8 *Broadway on the Ohio* 8 p.m.

Home of the annual spring Humana Festival of New American Plays, one of the nation's foremost new-works festivals, **Actors Theatre of Louisville** (316 West Main Street; 502-584-1205; actorstheatre.org) not only provides a rigorous testing ground for new talent, but shows well-acted plays for most of the year. The festival introduced Pulitzer Prize-winning plays including *Dinner With Friends* and *Crimes of the Heart* and has sent an impressive cadre of graduates on to Broadway. If nothing at Actors Theatre

strikes your fancy, check out the **Kentucky Center for the Arts** (501 West Main Street; 502-562-0100; kentuckycenter.org), which hosts touring productions as well as performances by the Louisville Orchestra and the Louisville Ballet.

9 *Borne Back Ceaselessly* 10:30 p.m.

The college crowd and some of their elders party at Louisville's overwrought, underthought **Fourth Street Live**, an urban mall featuring clubs, bars, and places like T.G.I. Fridays and a Hard Rock Cafe. Take a few steps from that chaos, however, and discover the wonderfully worn **Old Seelbach Bar** (500 Fourth Street; 502-585-3200; seelbachhilton.com). It's rumored that when F. Scott Fitzgerald was a young military officer stationed in Louisville, he would while away the hours at this stately lounge directly off the Seelbach Hotel's grand lobby. The hotel itself has a cameo in the film version of *The Great Gatsby*, but Fitzgerald didn't highlight the bar in his masterpiece, preferring to keep the best for himself. At least that's how the local story goes. Whatever the reason, it's better this way.

SUNDAY

10 *A Walk in the Park* 10 a.m.

Wake up with a jolt from the local favorite **Heine Brothers' Coffee** (1295 Bardstown Road;

502-456-5108; heinebroscoffee.com). This location shares a passageway with one of the last great bookstores, **Carmichael's** (1295 Bardstown Road; 502-456-6950; carmichaelsbookstore.com). Feel free to amble back and forth while you prepare

ABOVE You can try out the punching bag, but the Muhammad Ali Center isn't all about boxing. Multimedia presentations contextualize the life and career of Ali, who grew up in Louisville, within the civil rights struggle.

OPPOSITE At Jack Fry's, a legendary haven for bootleggers and bookies, diners now find a more genteel atmosphere.

for **Cherokee Park**. Opened in 1892, Cherokee was one of Frederick Law Olmsted's last and wildest creations — think Prospect Park in the foothills of Appalachia. Park near Hogan's Fountain and you can explore the nearly 400 acres of trails, hills, and meadows.

11 *Cave Hill* 1 p.m.
Colonel Harland Sanders — yes, that Colonel Sanders — lies alongside local luminaries like George Rogers Clark, the city's founder, at **Cave Hill Cemetery** (701 Baxter Avenue; 502-451-5630; cavehillcemetery.com), a lush Victorian-era graveyard that offers, unsurprisingly, a peaceful respite amid the bustle of the Highlands neighborhood. Before leaving, go native and leave a spork or a packet of ketchup at the Colonel's Doric-columned grave site, a memorial to his fried chicken fame.

THE BASICS

Fly into Louisville International Airport or drive into town on interstate highways 64, 65, or 71.

You will need a car to get around.

21C Museum Hotel
700 West Main Street
502-217-6300
21chotel.com
$$$
A highly rated hotel-art gallery with 9,000 square feet of exhibition space.

The Brown Hotel
335 West Broadway
502-583-1234
brownhotel.com
$$
Grand old hotel open since 1923.

The Seelbach-Hilton
500 Fourth Street
502-585-3200
seelbachhilton.com
$$$$
A Louisville classic.

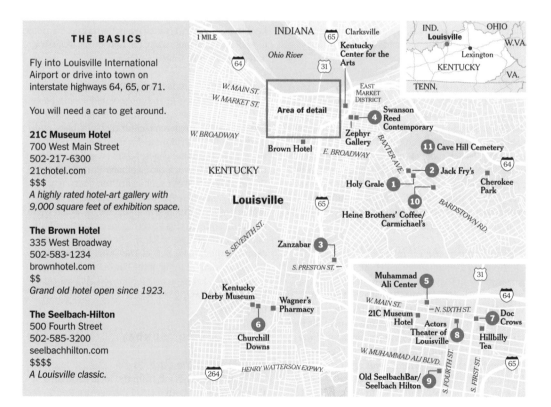

Nashville

Nashville, Tennessee, isn't nicknamed Music City for nothing. Singers, songwriters, and pickers — not to mention their toe-tapping admirers — have been pouring in for decades. This is where country music lives and breathes, but Nashville is a big tent for good music, nurturing generations of musicians playing rock and alt-country, R & B, and even jazz and classical. While it revels in its country roots, there's a new beat in once-sleepy neighborhoods like East Nashville and 12 South that thrive with lively bars, stylish restaurants, and a young, eclectic crop of music makers, churning out everything from bluegrass to punkabilly.

— BY KEITH MULVIHILL AND TAYLOR HOLLIDAY

FRIDAY

1 *Get the Picture* 4 p.m.

For an introduction to downtown, traditionally country music central, stroll along the Cumberland River and over the Shelby Avenue bridge, where the view is superb. Heading uptown along Broadway, don't miss **Hatch Show Print** (316 Broadway; 615-256-2805; hatchshowprint.com), in business since 1879. A letterpress print shop and gallery, it displays and sells handmade copies of gems like "Dolly Parton and Her Family Traveling Band" and "In Person: B.B. King." Down the street, the **Ernest Tubb Record Shop** (417 Broadway; 615-255-7503; etrecordshop.com), where the original honky-tonk hero once broadcast his midnight radio jamboree, carries almost every classic country and bluegrass recording available. And close by is the Ryman Auditorium, the original Grand Ole Opry stage.

2 *Green Cuisine* 7 p.m.

Take a short drive and relax away from downtown's crowds. Earthy hues set a pleasant, unfussy vibe at **Tayst** (2100 21st Avenue South; 615-383-1953; taystrestaurant.com; $$), which bills itself as Nashville's first restaurant to earn certification from the Green Restaurant Association, a nonprofit based in Boston that promotes environmentally friendly restaurants. Look for seasonal American dishes from local farms; one autumn menu included pork brined with maple syrup served with wild rice, chestnuts, and spicy cranberries. A smartly dressed after-work crowd mingles at the wine bar.

3 *Do the Grapevine* 9:30 p.m.

In the mid-1990s, *The Wildhorse Saloon Dance Show* on the Nashville Network inspired legions of viewers to learn the Boot Scootin' Boogie and the Watermelon Crawl. Today, the sprawling **Wildhorse Saloon** (120 Second Avenue North; 615-902-8200; wildhorsesaloon.com) continues to draw eager crowds. That there are more flip-flops than cowboy boots is a tad disheartening, but the enthusiasm for line dancing doesn't appear to have waned. You don't know how to do a grapevine? No problem. Check the schedule and arrive early for a lesson when an instructor walks everyone through the steps. You'll be kick-ball-change-stomp stomping like a pro.

SATURDAY

4 *Music Box* 10:30 a.m.

Hundreds of country hits were recorded at **Studio B** (1611 Roy Acuff Place), a drab cinderblock building in the historic Music Row district, where RCA legends like Elvis, Roy Orbison, and Dolly Parton sang their hearts out. The unglamorous space looks largely unchanged from when it was shuttered in 1977. Many visiting music fans haven't even heard of the studio let alone realize that it's one of the last vestiges of country music's golden years. The **Country Music**

OPPOSITE The Ryman Auditorium downtown.

RIGHT A mural fades downtown, but a younger, dynamic Nashville, rich in new and old music, is only blocks away.

ABOVE The Beaux Arts lobby of the century-old Hermitage Hotel in downtown Nashville.

BELOW Browsing at Grimey's New & Preloved Music.

Hall of Fame (222 Fifth Avenue South; 615-416-2001; countrymusichalloffame.org) offers hourlong tours of the studio. Piano players may be invited to tickle the ivories of the original Steinway grand piano.

5 *Fire Bird* 1 p.m.

"You can't handle it," a woman at **Prince's Hot Chicken Shack** (123 Ewing Drive; 615-226-9442; $), told one group of newbies who tried to order the "medium" spicy fried chicken. This long-revered spot serves four variations of its exceptional dish: mild, medium, hot, and extra hot. Order at your peril. The moist flesh is marinated and enveloped in a spicy rub before it's fried, so the hotness runs deep. Never mind the hole-in-the-wall décor; the savory hellfire is the draw—that, and the terrific sides of baked beans, coleslaw, and oh-so-sweet chess pie.

6 *Popsicles and Fringe* 3 p.m.

Cool off your first-degree burn at **Las Paletas** (2905 12th Avenue South; 615-386-2101), a small storefront that makes popsicles from fresh fruit and vegetables like honeydew, avocado, or hibiscus. Known simply as 12 South, 12th Avenue South is a trendy, tree-lined neighborhood packed with boutiques, cafes, and bars. You'll also find **Katy K Designs** (2407 12th Avenue South; 615-297-4242; katyk.com), a vintage clothing shop that specializes in country western wear from Johnny Cash black to Dollyesque showstoppers. A clutch of antiques shops including the **Eighth Avenue Antique Mall** (2015 Eighth Avenue South; 615-279-9922) is nearby. If it's indie recordings you crave, gems can be found at **Grimey's New & Preloved Music** (1604 Eighth Avenue South; 615-254-4801; grimeys.com).

7 *Opryland or Not* 7 p.m.

If country is calling, you'll find the sometimes corny, sometimes brilliant, but always endearing Grand Ole Opry most weekends several miles from

downtown at **Opryland** (2804 Opryland Drive; 615-871-6779; opry.com). Country legends, has-beens, stars, and wannabes all show up for this broadcast, the world's longest-running radio show. If you want more adventurous live music, hop over to East Nashville, a trendy neighborhood with a bevy of newer venues. Start off at the **Family Wash** (2038 Greenwood Avenue; 615-226-6070; familywash.com; $) where you can dig into tasty shepherd's pie, traditional or veggie. The alt-country, alt-rock, alt-folk acts start at 9 p.m.; the alt-crowd kicks back with locally brewed Yazoo beers. Next, head a few minutes down the road to the **5 Spot** (1006 Forrest Avenue; 615-650-9333; the5spotlive.com), where 20-somethings groove to live rock, country, or rockabilly.

8 *Southern Comfort* 11 p.m.

If your ears need a rest, grab a stool at the **Patterson House** (1711 Division Street; 615-636-7724; thepattersonnashville.com), a trendy mahogany-lined bar. Its creative libations have included a bacon-infused old-fashioned and the Juliet and Romeo, made with gin, rosewater, angostura bitters,

mint, and a sliver of cucumber. Dark wood and dim chandeliers make for a seductive backdrop.

SUNDAY

9 *Alt-Brunch* 9 a.m.

The menu may not list Southern good-ole-boy favorites, but there's nothing persnickety about **Marché Artisan Foods** (1000 Main Street; 615-262-1111; marcheartisanfoods.com; $$) in East Nashville, a bistro and market that fills a former boat showroom. The space has a homey vibe thanks to enticing display cases filled with baked goods, and a few family-size wooden tables. Standouts include the quiche with sausage and provolone.

ABOVE The antebellum mansion at Belle Meade Plantation, six miles outside of Nashville.

RIGHT Pastries for sale at Marché Artisan Foods, a bakery and bistro in East Nashville.

10 *Horsey Set* 11 a.m.

Before Nashville was known for its music, life here was moved by melodies both sweet and lowdown. Relive those antebellum days at **Belle Meade Plantation** (5025 Harding Pike; 615-356-0501; bellemeadeplantation.com), a 30-acre estate six miles from downtown. The centerpiece is a grand Greek-revival mansion completed in 1853, with a labyrinth of colorful rooms. In its heyday, the plantation was one of the most prosperous and successful

thoroughbred farms around. Portraits of muscular stallions grace the walls. In the library, visitors can view the silver-capped hooves of Iroquois, in 1881 the first American horse to win the English Derby. A posh carriage house, sobering slave quarters, and an 18th-century log cabin dot the lush grounds. Nashville's popularity may spring from country hits, but its cultural history offers a whole lot more.

ABOVE Hatch Show Print, a prominent maker of country music posters for generations.

OPPOSITE Dolly Parton, Elvis Presley, and Roy Orbison all sang their hearts out for recordings made in Studio B, in the historic Music Row district.

THE BASICS

Several carriers serve the Nashville airport, a 15-minute drive from downtown.

If you're not driving your own car, rent one.

Hermitage Hotel
231 Sixth Avenue North
615-244-3121
thehermitagehotel.com
$$$
An updated Nashville classic. Romantic Beaux-Arts lobby.

Hutton Hotel
1808 West End Avenue
615-340-9333
huttonhotel.com
$$
New, centrally located, smoke-free, and eco-friendly.

Union Station Hotel
1001 Broadway
615-726-1001
unionstationhotelnashville.com
$$
Ultramodern rooms in a former train station.

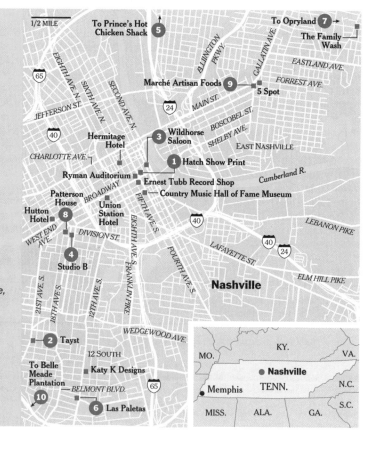

Memphis

You've worn Memphis's cotton, moved to its rhythm, sung its blues. Elvis Presley found his sound in this bluff city; B.B. King took his name, the Beale Street Blues Boy, from its 1940s entertainment district. "Home of the blues," the city now likes to trumpet. "Birthplace of rock 'n' roll." But these cultural revolutions, and the African-American milieu that spawned them, got no respect until Elvis died in 1977 and the city was inundated by grieving fans spending green money. Soon, Memphis began the urban-renewed version of Beale Street — its answer to Bourbon Street, sans the nudie shows — which over the years has become more like frat row. But deep blues do still exist in Memphis. You just have to dig deep to find them. — BY ROBERT GORDON

FRIDAY

1 *Three Little Words* 3 p.m.

Discussions about Memphis barbecue, even among friends, can lead to fisticuffs. Stop at **Payne's** (1762 Lamar Avenue; 901-272-1523; $) on your way in from the airport. It's a former service station, cavernous and spare. In Memphis, barbecue means pork shoulder, pulled from the bone or chopped and served with hot sauce or mild, with a dollop of cole slaw on top. The slaw is essential, as the perfect sandwich — i.e., Payne's — is a matter not only of taste but also of texture. "One chopped hot," you say at the counter, and three little words have never meant so much. The meat is succulent and tender; the mustardy slaw seeps into the tangy sauce. Don't worry. The sandwich isn't big enough to spoil dinner.

2 *It Came from Memphis* 5 p.m.

As Elvis would assure us, the world does indeed look great from inside a '55 Cadillac. See for yourself on Tad Pierson's three-hour **Greatest Hits** tour (901-527-8870; americandreamsafari.com; $200 for a party of one to five people). He picks you up — usually at the Peabody hotel (149 Union Avenue), although other arrangements may be made — in his refurbished Caddy and shows you the opulence and poverty of the city and its famous recording studios: Sun, home to Howling Wolf and Elvis; Stax, where Booker T. and the MG's backed Otis Redding; Hi, where Al Green recorded his sultry hits. In the entrepreneurial spirit of the city that brought you Holiday Inns and self-serve supermarkets, Mr. Pierson also peddles his Memphis Mary, a bloody mary mix with barbecue sauce. Get you some.

3 *You Said You Was High Class* 8:30 p.m.

There's a lot of grease in your future, so tonight it's dine fancy. **Mollie Fontaine** (679 Adams Avenue; 901-524-1886; molliefontainelounge.com; $$-$$$), a stylish bar and restaurant, fills two floors of a Victorian house where the soul songwriter Dan Penn — "Do Right Woman," "Cry Like a Baby" — once had his studio. Songs still float in the air, and patrons are as likely as the local greats — Di Anne Price included — to be playing them on the bar's piano. The menu of small plates mingles eclectic selections like lamb souvlaki and Spanish-style garlic shrimp with upscaled versions of sliders and fish fry.

4 *Nothin' but the Blues* 10:30 p.m.

It would be easy to hit Beale Street (if you do go, look for the soul performers James Govan or FreeWorld), but you came to Memphis for deep blues. Drive to **Wild Bill's** (1580 Vollintine Avenue; 901-726-5473), a storefront juke joint in a crumbling shopping strip. The room is deep and narrow, with snapshots of revelers tacked to the walls. Beer is served in quarts on long community tables, and when the dance floor fills up, folks shake it in the aisles. The band evolves and revolves; these players have backed Albert King and B.B. King, played world tours and dirt-floor hovels, and they'll transport you back in time, a real good time.

SATURDAY

5 *Hot Water Cornbread* 9:30 a.m.

Ease in with a Memphis Mary in your room before facing the harsh sun outside. Then hop the Main Street Trolley (matatransit.com), jumping off at Market Avenue to duck into **Alcenia's** (317 North Main Street; 901-523-0200; alcenias.com; $). B.J. — Alcenia's daughter — hugs everyone, and she usually serves hot water cornbread while you wait for your food.

OPPOSITE Beale Street now courts a party crowd, but deep blues still exist in Memphis.

You can't make a bad choice: options include salmon croquettes, dense pancakes, and sublime fried green tomatoes. Service can be slow, but this morning you're probably not moving too fast anyway.

6 *Soul, Man* 11 a.m.

Last night you lived the music, today you'll learn it. The headset tour at the **Memphis Rock 'n' Soul Museum** (191 Beale Street, in the FedExForum; 901-205-2533; memphisrocknsoul.org) includes original interviews and great music, evoking Memphis as a crossroads that bred new ideas and sounds. Look for an exhibit about Sputnik Monroe, a white wrestler who used his black fan base to integrate the city auditorium in the '50s. Then drive to the **Stax Museum of American Soul Music** (926 East McLemore Avenue; 901-946-2535; staxmuseum.com), an institution of a completely different nature — it has a dance floor, you dig? Stax was a studio and record label from 1957 to 1975, home of Isaac Hayes, Sam & Dave, the Staples Singers, and Albert King. There are more short, fun films than you can absorb in one visit, and you'll exit (into the gift shop) snapping your fingers.

7 *Memphis Soul Stew* 3 p.m.

You're hungry, you're in Soulsville USA — time for some soul food. The **Four Way** (998 Mississippi Boulevard; 901-507-1519; $) has been serving heaping portions for decades. The tender catfish is salted to perfection and fried in a crispy crust; the fried chicken is among the best in the South. Even if you're full, leaving without tasting the lemon meringue pie would be a tragedy.

ABOVE The Rock 'n' Soul Museum evokes Memphis as a crossroads that bred new ideas and sounds.

RIGHT Drinks in the piano bar at Mollie Fontaine, a stylish spot occupying two floors of a Victorian house where the soul songwriter Dan Penn once had his studio.

OPPOSITE The Mississippi River at Memphis.

8 *Find the Vinyl* 4:30 p.m.

There's good record hunting in Memphis — blues, rock 'n' roll, soul, indies. Start at **Goner Records** (2152 Young Avenue; 901-722-0095; goner-records.com) or nearby **Shangri-La Records** (1916 Madison Avenue; 901-274-1916; shangri.com). Both double as indie labels and have achieved national attention with regional artists, including the late garage rocker Jay Reatard, Harlan T. Bobo, and the Grifters. At Goner, look for the mini-shrine to Elvis impersonators. **Audiomania** (1698 Madison Avenue; 901-278-1166) has a deeper jazz and soul collection.

9 *Rollin' on the River* 6 p.m.

Park anywhere on Front Street downtown and take a few steps to the **Riverwalk**, a footpath carved into the bluffs along the Mississippi River. Evenings don't always cool down, but the whiff of magnolia and the sight of a tug pushing a massive load upstream will inspire the Huck Finn in anyone. During May weekends, Memphians throng the riverbank for events — a music festival, a barbecue contest, a symphony (memphisinmay.org).

10 *Night of Many Sounds* 9 p.m.

The cocktail is the concoction at the **Cove** (2559 Broad Avenue; 901-730-0719; thecovememphis.com). Disappear into an overstuffed leatherette booth and float away on the Blue Steel — tequila, just enough curacao to make it glow, and a lemon twist. Catch upcoming locals and some of the better indie bands here, or drift not far to the **Hi-Tone Café** (1913 Poplar Avenue; 901-278-8663; hitonememphis.com), where

higher-profile acts perform. The Hi-Tone is in the location of the former dojo where Elvis got his black belt; there's a photo over the bar. If you want a D.J. who's as likely to play Rufus Thomas as the latest dance hit, sail back downtown to the **Hollywood Disco** (115 Vance Avenue; 901-528-9313; hollywooddisco.com), and put on your b-b-boogie shoes.

SUNDAY

11 *Love, Happiness, Breakfast* 10 a.m.

The soul food on the menu at the **Rev. Al Green's Full Gospel Tabernacle Church** (787 Hale Road; algreenmusic.com/fullgospeltabernacle.html) is purely of the intangible kind. Even though he has a rejuvenated pop career, the reverend makes it home for more Sundays than he misses. He's as likely to break out into "Take Me to the River" as a psalm. Visitors are welcome, appropriate dress encouraged. Services start at 11:15, but first grab a sweet-potato-pancake breakfast with eggs and grits at the **Arcade Restaurant** (540 South Main Street; 901-526-5757; arcaderestaurant.com; $), across from the train station. In Jim Jarmusch's film *Mystery Train*, Elvis reappears at the Arcade. Keep your eyes open.

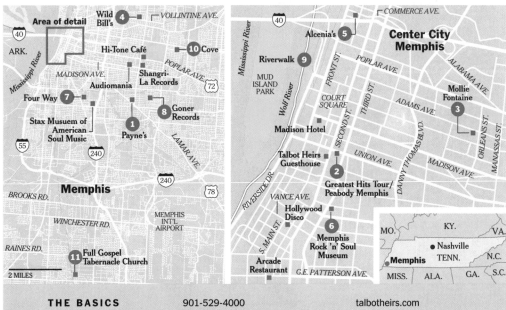

THE BASICS

Memphis International Airport is served by major airlines. About the only transportation worse than taxis in Memphis is the bus service. Rent a car.

The Peabody Memphis
149 Union Avenue
901-529-4000
peabodymemphis.com
$$$
Refurbished grand old downtown hotel, dripping with tradition and known for its resident ducks.

The Talbot Heirs Guesthouse
99 South Second Street
901-527-9772
talbotheirs.com
$$-$$$
One of Memphis's best secrets.

Madison Hotel
79 Madison Avenue
901-333-1200
madisonhotelmemphis.com
$$$
Lots of character.

Clarksdale

For decades, Clarksdale, Mississippi, has been more famous for the musicians who left than for anyone who stayed. The electric blues masters Muddy Waters and John Lee Hooker, the rhythm and blues pioneer Ike Turner and the soul man Sam Cooke are just a few of the refugees who made a hard turn onto Highway 61 north and never looked back. They sought greater opportunity, but also were fleeing poverty and the Jim Crow South. Want and hardship still haunt Clarksdale—those shotgun shacks are not for nostalgic show—but clarksdaletourism.com beckons visitors with a blue guitar and two highway signs that mark the mythic crossroads where, it is said, the bluesman Robert Johnson sold his soul to ol' Scratch in exchange for a few otherworldly guitar licks. Clarksdale's downtown is just a few square blocks—fine for a city of about 20,000—but its legend, as a kiln for shaping the blues, resonates worldwide. (And you never know when you might stumble over the ghost of Tennessee Williams, who spent much of his childhood here.)

— BY ROBERT GORDON

FRIDAY

1 *Blues Highway* 3 p.m.

Unless you pilot a crop duster (like some of the locals), you'll fly into Memphis and rent a car to get to Clarksdale. The drive south will take you through cotton fields and cypress swamps and is dotted with small towns—Lula, Robinsonville, and Tunica. An old diner there, the **Blue & White** (1355 Highway 61 north, Tunica; 662-363-1371; $), serves sublime onion rings in a delicate but crunchy batter, and homemade pies. Allow a leisurely hour and a half for the 75-mile drive. When you find yourself swaying to the soulful sounds of **WROX** (1450 AM and 92.1 FM; wroxradio.com), you're getting close.

2 *Picking Cotton Not Required* 5 p.m.

The **Hopson Plantation** is where the mechanical cotton picker was unveiled in 1941, and it is again on the cutting edge—this time with cultural tourism. The **Shack Up Inn** consists of six former sharecropper shacks, each transformed into a guesthouse that sleeps three or four. Yes, there is indoor plumbing (and kitchenettes). The contrast of the shacks' down-at-the-heels histories and their contemporary coziness can, at first, feel presumptuous and like a form of exploitation. One guestbook comment read: "Negrophilia: Commodification: Everything but the burden. Thanks!" But the silence and the breeze sneaking through the shacks' open doors make them a profound way to experience the Mississippi Delta. The **Cotton Gin Inn** recently opened on the same site: five hotel rooms built into an old cotton gin building.

3 *The Clarksdale Redemption* 7 p.m.

Just as you've become accustomed to the sense of being somewhere else, step into **Madidi** (164 Delta Avenue; 662-627-7724; madidires.com; $$$), a restaurant and cosmopolitan oasis. Entrees focus on urbane choices like rack of lamb or duck a l'orange, but starters may include regional flavors like frog legs or shrimp and grits. Madidi is partly owned by Morgan Freeman, who lives in nearby Charleston. After dinner, stroll through the small downtown to Freeman's other venture: **Ground Zero Blues Club** (364 Delta Avenue; 662-621-9009; groundzerobluesclub.com). A former cotton warehouse, Ground Zero is Clarksdale's top blues spot. The local favorites include Super Chikan, Jimbo Mathus (former leader of Squirrel Nut Zippers), the Deep Cuts, and Anthony Sherard—tomorrow's bluesman playing today—and his band, Big A and the All Stars.

OPPOSITE The Delta Amusement Blues Cafe serves a conventional breakfast, but its name honors Clarksdale's legacy as home of the blues.

BELOW Authentic blues at the Ground Zero Blues Club.

homes are nearby. Ms. Cutrer, an eccentric party-giver, fascinated a young neighborhood boy named Tom Williams, who one day became Tennessee and the writer of *A Streetcar Named Desire*. Blanche, of course, remained accustomed to the finer things.

SATURDAY

4 *Back-Door Museum* 9 a.m.

Breakfast at the **Delta Amusement Blues Cafe** (348 Delta Avenue; 662-624-4040; $) isn't anything you can't get on a grill elsewhere, but the sense of small-town intrigue is straight out of Eudora Welty. You can hear the laughing and cursing over poker and dominos even when the games aren't being played. Walk out the back door to the **Delta Blues Museum** (1 Blues Alley; 662-627-6820; deltabluesmuseum.org). Alluringly low-tech, it delivers not only the music but also the culture that produced it. Located in a former freight depot, the museum houses Muddy Waters's childhood cabin. Step inside and feel the blues falling down like rain. Nearby is **Cat Head Delta Blues & Folk Art** (252 Delta Avenue; 662-624-5992; cathead.biz), a shop stuffed with Southern creations.

5 *My Meal Is Red Hot* 11 a.m.

Robert Johnson sang about them in "They're Red Hot," and you can savor the heritage of Delta hot tamales at **Hicks Tamales & BBQ Shop** (305 South State Street; 662-624-9887). Creamy cornmeal mashes with spicy beef centers, they're simmered for hours inside a cornhusk. Unwrap, eat, then whoop. For barbecue, locals favor **Abe's** (616 North State Street; 662-624-9947) and **Big Jim's** (1700 North State Street), a shack the size of a pickup where a summer treat is the "koolickle": cucumbers steeped in cherry, grape, or strawberry Kool-Aid.

6 *Of Indians and Desire* Noon

Even for those who know Clarksdale well, **Robert Birdsong's tour** ($60 for three hours, custom tours available; 662-624-6051; mississippimojo@yahoo.com) gives the place new life. Standing on the bank of the Sunflower River, where two Indian trading paths met, Birdsong lectures on an 1880 landslide that exposed a tribal burial site, attracting a Smithsonian excavation team. He then ties those events to the town's founder, John Clark, and his daughter Blanche Cutrer, whose

7 *A Fine Mess* 3 p.m.

Hightail it 15 miles north to Friar's Point, a blocklong town that peaked in the early 1900s but has clung to life like morning dew on sweet potato vines. The **North Delta Museum** (700 Second Street; 662-383-2233 or 645-5063), at the base of the curving Mississippi River levee, comes across as the family attic given a rarefied name. Holdings include Civil War and World War I memorabilia and American Indian displays. Across the street is Hirsberg's, an old-time dry-goods store; Robert Johnson played from that bench out front.

8 *Faulkner, Twitty, Crayfish* 6 p.m.

In the middle of somebody's nowhere, you are near an unusual fine-dining experience for anybody. In 1926, an Elks Lodge was built on Moon Lake in Dundee, attracting local gamblers. The place was owned by Tennessee Williams's family and later by relatives of Conway Twitty (who was born in Friar's Point); William Faulkner used to frequent it. Since the mid-70s, it has been **Uncle Henry's Place** (5860 Moon Lake Road; 662-337-2757; unclehenrysplace.com; $$-$$$), run by George Wright, its chef, and his mother, Sarah, the resident historian. The food reflects their Louisiana roots (look for crayfish étouffée), but their talk is local.

9 *Rust Never Sleeps* 9 p.m.

It's a 25-minute drive back to Clarksdale, and time to check in at **Red's** (395 Sunflower Avenue) for some deep local flavor. The outside is strewn with rusted grills. And inside, the live music will push you toward abandon.

SUNDAY

10 *Sunday, Coming Down* 9:30 a.m.

Another comment from the Shack Up Inn guest book: "Great fried shrimp at Ramon's. T-Model Ford at Red's, Wiley and the Checkmates at Ground Zero.

Try fried grits with honey. Learn to take it slower."
Sound advice and, faced with Clarksdale's blue laws,
you don't have much choice. Try breakfast at the
Shady Nook (16774 Highway 61 north; 662-621-1525),
a truck-stop cafeteria on the north side of town.
And be sure to chat with other guests passing through
the shacks' lobby, which is owner Bill Talbot's
living room.

11 *Take Me to the River* 11 a.m.
     The **Quapaw Canoe Company** (291 Sunflower
Avenue; 662-627-4070 or 902-7841; island63.com),
named for a regional Indian tribe, does for the
Mississippi River what Robert Birdsong does for the
city. Trips can vary from an outing of a couple hours

to several weeks. John Ruskey, one of Quapaw's
guides, lives in a house once owned by the Wingfields,
where the missus was known for her menagerie of
glass animals; it's also the **Catalpa House** bed-and-
breakfast (110 Catalpa Street; 662-627-5621).

OPPOSITE AND ABOVE The converted sharecropper shacks
of the Shack Up Inn have the comforts their original
occupants lacked, but remain a link to the hardscrabble
life that fostered the deeply emotional Delta blues.

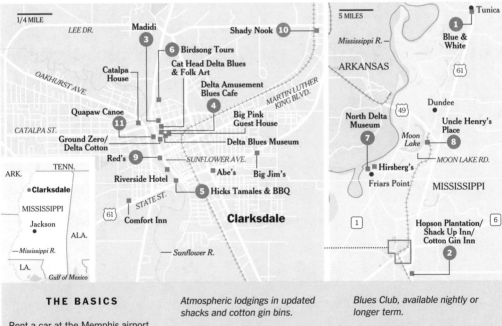

THE BASICS

Rent a car at the Memphis airport
and drive south on Highway 61.

Shack Up Inn and Cotton Gin Inn
001 Commissary Circle
662-624-8329
shackupinn.com
$

Atmospheric lodgings in updated
shacks and cotton gin bins.

**Delta Cotton Company
Apartments**
387 Delta Avenue, on Blues Alley
662-645-9366
groundzerobluesclub.com
$-$$
Upstairs from the Ground Zero

Blues Club, available nightly or
longer term.

Riverside Hotel
615 Sunflower Avenue
662-624-9163
$
*Former hospital for blacks where
Bessie Smith died in 1937 after
a car accident.*

Oxford

William Faulkner was born over in New Albany. But Oxford, Mississippi, claims him as its own, for he honed fictional Yoknapatawpha County from the people and places of surrounding Lafayette County. Named for Oxford, England, in a successful bid to lure Mississippi's liberal arts university, this town of about 20,000 sprawls out from the courthouse, described in Faulkner's 1951 novel Requiem for a Nun *as "brooding, symbolic, and ponderable, tall as cloud, solid as rock, dominating all." Faulkner still matters here. A majestic bronze statue of him, resting on a bench, pipe in hand, flanks the entrance to City Hall. The local temple of intellect, Square Books, stocks what seems like every blessed thing he wrote. And his home, Rowan Oak, went through a multimillion-dollar refurbishing and is open for tours. Though the courthouse square he knew — ringed by hardware stores and barbershops — is now the domain of boutiques and cigar boîtes, the local underclass of writers, artists, and graduate students remains a vigilant steward of the town's reputation as a velvet ditch for ne'er-do-wells.*
— BY JOHN T. EDGE

FRIDAY

1 *Nobel Blues* 4 p.m.

At the heart of the University of Mississippi campus, on the top floor of the **J. D. Williams Library**, a literary-cultural archive and a blues archive (662-915-7408; olemiss.edu) co-exist. James Meredith, the black man who integrated the campus as a student in 1962, donated his papers to Ole Miss, so you can see the note he received from Rosa Parks in support of his efforts. That is Faulkner's Nobel Prize over in the corner, swaddled in purple velvet. And B. B. King's personal collection is here, too. Thanks to a staff that understands how these collections complement one another, you will also see displays like a signed copy of Elmore Leonard's Mississippi-centered 2002 novel *Tishomingo Blues* alongside a 78-r.p.m. record of the same name, recorded in 1926 by Peg Leg Howell.

2 *Drinking with the Lions* 6 p.m.

Want to stalk a literary lion? The second-story bar at the **City Grocery** restaurant (152 Courthouse Square; 662-232-8080; citygroceryonline.com; $$$) is the place for it. Jack Pendarvis drinks Manhattans

and other fancy-pants cocktails here. Tom Franklin favors Bud Lights. Even if the literati are not around, you can ogle the brass plaques that are nailed to the bar when the owner decides that regulars have earned their stripes. The prime perches are on the balcony overlooking the square; they're scarce, so get here early. When you're ready for dinner, descend the staircase at the back and enter the restaurant, a white-tablecloth affair in a onetime grocery. John Currence, the owner, is a gutsy cook and in the vanguard of new Southern cuisine.

3 *Shot and a Beer* 10 p.m.

Every college town needs a dank beer-and-a-shot bar; the **Blind Pig** (105 North Lamar Boulevard; 662-234-5119) does the job in Oxford. You might see a rocking local band, like Tyler Keith and the Preacher's Kids. Fair warning: Last calls on the weekend are 12:45 on Friday night and 11:45 on Saturday night.

SATURDAY

4 *Ginger Scones and Peacocks* 9 a.m.

The owner of **Bottletree Bakery** (923 Van Buren Avenue; 662-236-5000), Cynthia Gerlach, got her master's in Southern studies from the university's Center for the Study of Southern Culture, writing her thesis on B.F. Perkins, an Alabama painter known for his vividly colored peacocks. After a spell at the low-slung counter, it's hard to tell whether your morning buzz is born of the kinetic images that blanket the walls, the sugary punch of a candied ginger-studded scone, or the coffee that Gerlach imports from her hometown, Portland, Oregon.

5 *Square Stroll* 10 a.m.

Oxonians take pride in their literary heritage. They even elected Richard Howorth, proprietor of three storefront bookshops (squarebooks.com), their mayor for two terms. **Square Books** (160 Courthouse Square; 662-236-2262) is the place for a staggering array of signed firsts; **Off Square Books** (129 Courthouse Square; 662-236-2828) specializes in used

OPPOSITE Rowan Oak, William Faulkner's home. Oxford was thinly disguised as "Jefferson" in Faulkner's fiction.

thousands at the **Grove**, ten shady acres on campus. If it's one of the other 45 Saturdays of the year, you might find some serenity in a stroll under those same oak, elm, and magnolia trees. (Enter campus from the east, on University Avenue, and you'll soon see it on your right. For maximum effect, enter under an archway inscribed "Walk of the Champions.") Walk a bit farther, across the University Circle and behind the Lyceum, to find the **Civil Rights Monument**, a bronze statue of Meredith striding onto the campus in 1962.

8 *Visions of Plenty* 4 p.m.

The **Mary Buie collection** of the **University of Mississippi Museum** (University Avenue and North Fifth Street; 662-915-7073; museum.olemiss.edu) is a Grandma's attic showcase of curiosities (rings crafted from peach pits; hair from the tail of Robert E. Lee's horse, Traveler) as well as folk art (Luster Willis, Sultan Rogers) and choice modern art (William Eggleston, William Dunlap). It's also a great air-conditioned break after a campus walk on a hot day.

and remaindered; and **Jr.** (111 Courthouse Square; 662-236-2207) is for, well, juniors. Other square shops worthy of your wallet and eyes are the **Southside Gallery** (150 Courthouse Square; 662-234-9090; southsideartgallery.com), which exhibits photographers like Maude Schuyler Clay; **Amelia** (1006 Van Buren Avenue; 901-355-0311; ameliapresents.com), where craft meets design and intersects with cupcakes; and **Neilson's** (119 Courthouse Square; 662-234-1161; neilsons1839.com), a department store that has been in business since 1839.

9 *Country Roads and Eats* 7 p.m.

Time for a drive. Pilot your car southwest about eight miles on Taylor Road, and you will dead-end at the hamlet of Taylor. At the center of a shamble of storefronts stands **Taylor Grocery** (04-A County Road 338, Taylor; 662-236-1716; taylorgrocery.com; $-$$), a restaurant embellished with corrugated tin and

6 *Frill Pick Shooting* 1 p.m.

The **Ajax Diner** (118 Courthouse Square; 662-232-8880; ajaxdiner.net; $) fixes plate lunches built around meatloaf, chicken and gravy, fried catfish, and the like, accompanied by sweet potato casserole, mashed potatoes drenched in gravy, and butter beans swimming in a peppery "potlikker." The place is best appreciated on warm spring days when the step-through windows are thrown open. While waiting for lunch, do what the cool kids do: snag a frill-topped toothpick, load it into a plastic straw and send it blowgun-style into the ceiling tiles.

ABOVE The Mary Buie collection ranges from the gowns of belles to hair from the tail of Robert E. Lee's horse.

BELOW A porch-rocker view of Courthouse Square.

7 *The Grove* 2 p.m.

On seven or eight Saturday afternoons in fall, Oxford is transformed as alumni and adoring fans arrive for Ole Miss football. For hours before the game, they mingle, party, and get pumped up by the

graffiti. It may serve the best cornmeal-dusted catfish in this catfish-crazy state. Before you go in for dinner, take a walk around the town, where artists gather and shops and galleries sell their work.

SUNDAY

10 *A Different Kind of Benedict* 10 a.m.

Better known as a bar that books literate rock one night and a hippie jam band the next, **Proud Larry's** (211 South Lamar Boulevard; 662-236-0050; proudlarrys.com; $) emerges from six days of beer and sacrilege to serve late-morning fare to churchgoers. Standard-bearers include fat biscuits in sausage gravy and the Larry Benedict, two English muffins

topped with sausage patties and poached eggs and drenched in Tabasco-spiked hollandaise sauce.

11 *Mr. Bill's Place* 12:30 p.m.

Locals once took pride in telling visitors that **Rowan Oak** (913 Old Taylor Road; 662-234-3284; rowanoak.com), William Faulkner's home on Old Taylor Road, remained much as it was when he died in 1962. His muddy boots and his Underwood typewriter sat where he had left them. But eventually restoration took place. Tours don't start until 1 p.m., but arrive early to wander the grounds, stroll among the cedars that frame the front walk, and peer through the windows at the outline for *A Fable* scrawled on the wall of his study.

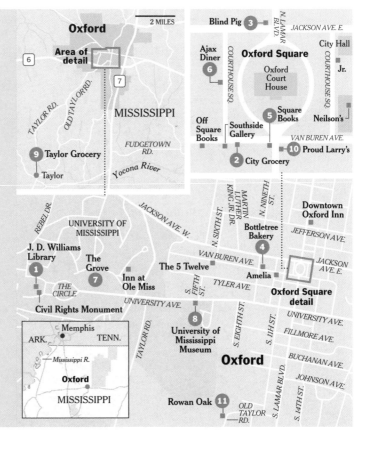

THE BASICS

Fly into Memphis International Airport, rent a car and drive the scenic route, Highway 78 East to Highway 7 South. Keep driving.

Downtown Oxford Inn
400 North Lamar Boulevard
662-234-3031
downtownoxfordinn.com
$$
Former Holiday Inn remodeled and retrofitted with oversize columns in a style one local critic called "RocoCola."

The 5 Twelve
512 Van Buren Avenue
662-234-8043
the512oxford.com
$$
Five-room inn in a red-brick manor house.

Inn at Ole Miss
Alumni Drive, University of Mississippi
662-234-2331
theinnatolemiss.com
$
Near the Grove on the Ole Miss campus.

Birmingham

In the golden days of rail travel, a sign proclaiming "Welcome to Birmingham, the Magic City" greeted passengers arriving at Terminal Station. Although the station is only a memory today, Alabama's largest city still retains a special ability to surprise the uninitiated —particularly for modern visitors who arrive with collective memories of the city's violent civil rights past. That past is certainly memorialized, but the city has plenty more to offer: enticing takes on Southern cuisine, a nationally acclaimed motorsports park, and upscale shopping opportunities.
— BY JIM NOLES

FRIDAY

1 *Standing Tall* 4 p.m.

In 1871, Birmingham was incorporated at the strategic juncture of two rail lines where local deposits of iron and coal would nurture the young city's iron furnaces. The founders' vision was so successful that when the city's Commerce Club was invited to dispatch a symbol of Birmingham to the 1904 World's Fair, it commissioned a cast-iron statue of **Vulcan**, the Roman god of the forge. Today, the impressive statue (1701 Valley View Drive; 205-933-1409; visitvulcan. com) stands in a park atop Red Mountain, offering an unmatched vista of Birmingham's downtown skyline to those who go up to visit it—and providing residents of downtown Homewood, south of the mountain, with a view of Vulcan's massive bare rump.

2 *Not Your Grandma's Grits* 6 p.m.

Highlands Bar & Grill (2011 11th Avenue South; 205-939-1400; highlandsbarandgrill.com; $$$), recognized by the James Beard Foundation as one of the country's best restaurants, owes its reputation to chef and owner Frank Stitt, who deftly combines fresh, rural ingredients and French-inspired technique. The restaurant's stone-ground baked grits, accented with Smoky Mountain-raised country ham, mushrooms, thyme, and Parmesan, have been a local favorite for years. Call ahead for a reservation, but arrive early for

a drink at the bar, where fresh oysters on the half-shell whet appetites for entrees like farm-raised lamb with fresh mint and sweet peas.

3 *All Work and All Play* 9 p.m.

The brainchild of Alan Hunter, one of MTV's original V.J.'s, **WorkPlay** (500 23rd Street South; 205-879-4773; workplay.com) is an entertainment complex that includes a live-music venue, a bar packed with a 20-something crowd, a professional sound stage, and even a suite of offices for creative professional types, all on the edge of Birmingham's warehouse district. The bar usually clears out when the live music starts next door, courtesy of acts ranging from the singer-songwriter Neko Case to the Southern rockers the Zac Brown Band. Intimacy is part of the appeal: a mere arm's length separates the musicians from the audience. Check WorkPlay's Web site for scheduled acts and to purchase tickets.

SATURDAY

4 *Continental's Breakfast* 8 a.m.

Just over the crest of Red Mountain, **Continental Bakery** (1909 Cahaba Road; 205-870-5584; birminghammenus.com/chezlulu) greets arrivals to English Village, a small commercial district on the edge of the affluent suburb of Mountain Brook. Order inside the narrow shop, where display cases lined with fresh baguettes, bread, and pastries conjure the ambience of Dijon rather than Dixie. Outside, claim a seat at a sidewalk table, pet a neighbor's dog, and enjoy a butter croissant.

OPPOSITE Vulcan, cast in iron, stands atop Red Mountain. The iron and steel industry built Birmingham.

RIGHT An after-work crowd at Highlands Bar & Grill.

5 *It Takes a Village* 10 a.m.

Just down the hill from English Village, Mountain Brook Village holds tony shops befitting the area's origins as a forested suburban refuge from the soot-spewing smokestacks of early industrial Birmingham. At **Table Matters** (2402 Montevallo Road; 205-879-0125; table-matters.com), shoppers brush shoulders as they search for gifts ranging from William Yeoward crystal to the Good Earth Pottery produced by the Mississippi craftsman Richie Watts. Nearby at **Etc. Jewelry and Accessories** (2726 Cahaba Road; 205-871-6747), husbands seek surreptitious guidance on the latest jewelry from the designer Priyadarshini Himatsingka or handbags from Monica Botkier.

6 *Good Golly Miss Myra* 12:30 p.m.

In any travel article discussing Alabama, you'd expect a reference to barbecue. Here it is. Although every Birmingham resident has a favorite, **Miss Myra's Pit Bar-B-Q** (3278 Cahaba Heights Road; 205-967-6004; missmyrasbbq.com; $) makes any aficionado's short list. The lunch crowd is steady, even into the early afternoon, as fragrant smoke wafts across the parking lot from the wide brick chimney. Inside, the décor of this former convenience store is mostly a celebration of the past glory of the Crimson Tide; a display of porcelain pigs donated by loyal customers offers its own homage to the restaurant's most delectable offerings. Pork and rib sandwiches and plates are available, of course, but Myra Grissom's signature white sauce (a concoction of mayo, pepper and vinegar) works particularly well on her chicken.

7 *A Monument to Injustice* 2 p.m.

Two very different museums offer equally compelling glimpses of Birmingham—one of its past, the other of its future. Across the street from the historic **Sixteenth Street Baptist Church** (site of the infamous bombing that killed four girls in 1963), the **Birmingham Civil Rights Institute** (520 16th Street North; 205-328-9696; bcri.org) tells the story of the civil rights movement in Alabama and beyond and provides a somber reminder of how far the city and the nation have come in four decades. The church itself, still serving a downtown congregation, offers tours Tuesday through Friday, and, by appointment only, on Saturdays (205-251-9402).

8 *Need for Speed* 4 p.m.

Twenty minutes east of town, in the rolling hills along the Cahaba River, the **Barber Vintage Motorsports Museum** (6030 Barber Motorsports Parkway; 205-699-7275; barbermuseum.org) hints at how Birmingham's future reputation might be cast. The museum claims the largest motorcycle collection in North America (more than 900 bikes in total) in an airy five-story display that feels as much like an art museum as a motor pool. The **Barber Motorsports Park** (barbermotorsports.com) is adjacent to the museum. Its creator, George Barber, likens its immaculately groomed grounds to "the Augusta of racetracks."

9 *Front Row Seats* 6 p.m.

Despite his restaurant's name, Chris Hastings, the chef and owner of the **Hot and Hot Fish Club** (2180 11th Court South; 205-933-5474; hotandhotfishclub.com; $$$), quickly recommended the pork-belly appetizer. "It will set your mind free," he said. The dish combined a melt-in-your-mouth fattiness with just the right amount of crispy skin. "I get my pork from Henry

Fudge, up in north Alabama," Hastings added. "The man's a pig genius." Apparently so. Hastings reserved similar enthusiasm for his simple grilled fish, on this partcular visit a pompano that just the day before it was served had been swimming in the Gulf of Mexico. It was served whole on a bed of couscous. Reservations are suggested, as are seats at the chef's counter, where conversation with fellow patrons flows naturally.

SUNDAY

10 *Brunch at the Park* 11 a.m.
Little Savannah (3811 Clairmont Avenue; 205-591-1119; birminghammenus.com/littlesavannah;

$$), on the edge of the historic Forest Park neighborhood, calls itself a "quaint neighborhood Southern Bistro"—an apt description. Orders of the cranberry-pecan cream cheese-filled French toast and the crab cake with bacon, creamed spinach, and a poached egg threatened to disrupt the peace one Sunday with a lively debate on which selection was better. Reservations recommended.

OPPOSITE ABOVE Half art museum, half motor pool, the Barber Vintage Motorsports Museum has 900 bikes.

OPPOSITE BELOW The Birmingham Civil Rights Institute is a reminder of how far the city has come since the infamous church bombing that killed four girls in 1963.

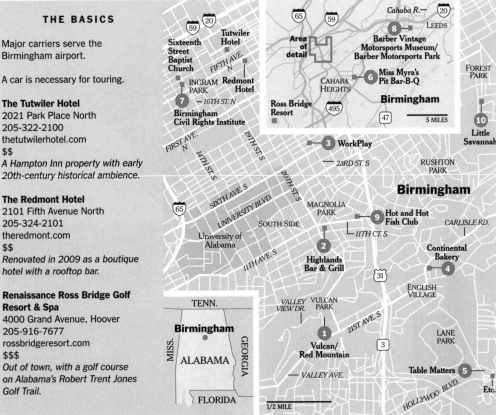

THE BASICS

Major carriers serve the Birmingham airport.

A car is necessary for touring.

The Tutwiler Hotel
2021 Park Place North
205-322-2100
thetutwilerhotel.com
$$
A Hampton Inn property with early 20th-century historical ambience.

The Redmont Hotel
2101 Fifth Avenue North
205-324-2101
theredmont.com
$$
Renovated in 2009 as a boutique hotel with a rooftop bar.

Renaissance Ross Bridge Golf Resort & Spa
4000 Grand Avenue, Hoover
205-916-7677
rossbridgeresort.com
$$$
Out of town, with a golf course on Alabama's Robert Trent Jones Golf Trail.

Montgomery

When the United Daughters of the Confederacy organized a Montgomery branch in 1896, its members named their chapter "Cradle of the Confederacy." Approximately a century later, veterans of the civil rights movement began referring to Alabama, and its capital, Montgomery, in particular, as the "birthplace of the civil rights movement." At a gooseneck bend in the Alabama River, this city of 200,000 delivers on both claims. A spate of museum building and downtown redevelopment now attract cultural tourists, but the transition has not wiped clean the contradictions. Drive south of downtown and, in the shadow of the Martin Luther King Jr. Expressway (Interstate 85), you will pass a sign for Taraland Learning Center. It's just a few blocks west of the intersection of Jefferson Davis and Rosa L. Parks Avenues.

— BY JOHN T. EDGE

FRIDAY

1 *Learning about Hank* 4 p.m.

Hank Williams, who was born near Garland, Alabama, is the city's favorite musical son. And the best place to get a bead on the man who, before his death at the age of 29 in 1953, wrote and recorded standards like "I'll Never Get Out of This World Alive," is the storefront **Hank Williams Museum** (118 Commerce Street; 334-262-3600; thehankwilliamsmuseum.com). View the baby blue Cadillac in which Williams died and artifacts like a selection of toothpicks pulled from one of his suits, a lime-fringed black shirt custom-made by Nudie's Rodeo Tailors, and the saddle he used for riding his horse, Hi-Life.

2 *Alabama Riverside* 8 p.m.

Call for directions to the **Capitol Oyster Bar** at the Montgomery Marina (617 Shady Street; 334-239-8958; capitoloysterbar.com; $), and you're still likely to get lost. But a short trek across a web of freight tracks and through the city's industrial areas brings you to the ideal time-worn perch for a sunset beer. Below are the slips of sailboats and cabin cruisers. In the

OPPOSITE A bronze Hank Williams strums perpetually across from the City Auditorium in Montgomery.

RIGHT The Cross Garden, one man's roadside obsession.

distance, barges ply the Alabama River. Stay for a casual dinner. The menu is simple (fried seafood platters, steak, cheeseburgers), but the setting is lulling and there may be some music.

3 *Jazz Underground* 11 p.m.

Keep the evening going at **Sous La Terre Downtown Underground** (82 Commerce Street; 334-265-2069), a private club set, true to its moniker, in a windowless basement. It usually opens around 11 p.m. and springs to life after midnight when a jazz piano player, Henry Pugh, takes the stage. Guests must apply for membership to enter, but you won't find that much of a barrier. The crowd is friendly and the jazz is the real thing.

SATURDAY

4 *Curbside Eating* 9 a.m.

Open since 1927, downtown's **Montgomery Curb Market** (1004 Madison Avenue; 334-263-6445; montgomeryal.gov/index.aspx?page=648) is an open-air shebang lighted by dangling bulbs and topped by a metal roof. In addition to produce, you'll find a heady array of baked goods. Hungry? Look for homemade sausage and cheese biscuits, fried peach pies, and miniature sweet potato pies.

5 *Old South* 10 a.m.

Dexter Avenue is only six blocks long, but it's the spine of a route from the site of Jefferson Davis's inauguration to the bus stop where Rosa Parks boarded for her fateful journey. Start an Old South morning atop Goat Hill, at the **Alabama State Capitol**

(600 Dexter Avenue; 334-242-3935; sos.state.al.us/OfficeOfSoS/CapitolTours.aspx), which is ringed by statuary and monuments that honor, among others, Dr. J. Marion Sims, who is called the father of modern gynecology. From the portico, where Davis took his oath as president of the Confederacy in 1861, George Wallace proclaimed in 1963, "Segregation now, segregation tomorrow, segregation forever." On the northern lawn rises a white marble memorial to the Confederacy. Detour one street south of Dexter Avenue and you stand in front of the **First White House of the Confederacy** (644 Washington Avenue; 334-242-1861; firstwhitehouse.org), the modest — and now musty — Italianate two-story building that Davis and his family called home in the aftermath of secession. The gift shop sells books and souvenirs including reproduction Confederate money.

6 *All American* 1 p.m.

Take a lunch break from history at **Chris' Hot Dogs** (138 Dexter Avenue; 334-265-6850; chrishotdogs.com), which has been selling the timeless American snack since 1917. The dogs come mustard-slathered and drenched in chili sauce. Snag a stool at the worn linoleum counter where some locals say Hank Williams sat and scribbled lyrics.

7 *New South* 2 p.m.

Advance to the 20th century, starting at the **Civil Rights Memorial** (400 Washington Avenue; splcenter.org/civil-rights-memorial), designed by Maya Lin and commissioned by the Southern Poverty Law Center, the group that bankrupted the United Klans of America. Water emerges from the core of a circular granite table, washing over the names of martyrs of the civil rights movement in what might be interpreted as absolution of the South's sins. Back on Dexter Avenue, the **Dexter Avenue King Memorial Baptist Church** (454 Dexter Avenue; 334-263-3970; dexterkingmemorial.org), where Martin Luther King Jr. rose to fame as leader of the Montgomery Improvement Association, stands out in red brick

among the white masonry of state government buildings. Founded by former slaves in 1877, it remains a church and also gives tours where docents explain the history. One comment about Vernon Johns, King's predecessor: "If he had led the movement, we'd all be dead — he wasn't one to turn the other cheek." The **Rosa L. Parks Library and Museum** (252 Montgomery Street; 334-241-8615; montgomery.troy.edu/rosaparks), at the spot where in 1955 Parks refused to give up her seat on a bus to a white passenger, has multimedia displays and uses special effects to take visitors on a simulated bus ride back in time.

8 *Pull the Trigger* 7 p.m.

A shotgun restaurant with a bar on the side and a trophy-size blue marlin arcing across the back wall, **Jubilee Seafood** (1057 Woodley Road; 334-262-6224; jubileeseafoodrestaurant.com; $$-$$$) serves up dishes like pecan-topped snapper and grilled sea bass with mushrooms and crabmeat. The Key lime pie is a comely whorl of citrus and meringue.

SUNDAY

9 *Brimstone in the Pines* 9 a.m.

Drive about 12 miles north on I-65 and a few miles west on Highway 82 toward Prattville, and take a left on Autauga County Road 86, also called Indian Hills Road. At a bend in the two-lane

blacktop, the **Cross Garden** erupts. Constructed as a testimony of Christian faith by W.C. Rice, who died in 2004, this folk art environment, set amid gullies rife with castoff appliances, warns, by way of hundreds of painted crosses, "Hell Is Hot, Hot, Hot!" and recalls Flannery O'Connor's observation that the South was a "Christ-haunted" place.

10 *Country-Fried Brunch* 10:45 a.m.

Wend back into town for an experience closer to the heavenly side. **Martin's Restaurant** (1796 Carter Hill Road; 334-265-1767; martinsrestaurant.org; $$) has been frying chickens and baking coconut meringue pies since 1940. It also does right by collard greens, candied yams, and string beans. But the best is the

simplest: corn muffins crisp and steaming with sweet corn flavor. Plan to arrive soon after they open at 10:45, or you'll spend your Sunday morning in line with the crowds that flock from nearby churches.

OPPOSITE ABOVE The Rosa Parks bus replica.

OPPOSITE BELOW The Civil Rights Monument.

ABOVE The Alabama State Capitol.

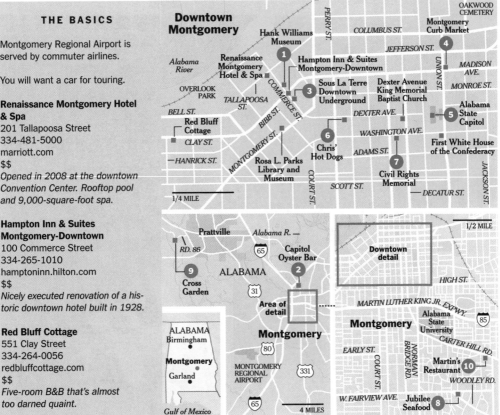

THE BASICS

Montgomery Regional Airport is served by commuter airlines.

You will want a car for touring.

Renaissance Montgomery Hotel & Spa
201 Tallapoosa Street
334-481-5000
marriott.com
$$
Opened in 2008 at the downtown Convention Center. Rooftop pool and 9,000-square-foot spa.

Hampton Inn & Suites Montgomery-Downtown
100 Commerce Street
334-265-1010
hamptoninn.hilton.com
$$
Nicely executed renovation of a historic downtown hotel built in 1928.

Red Bluff Cottage
551 Clay Street
334-264-0056
redbluffcottage.com
$$
Five-room B&B that's almost too darned quaint.

New Orleans

What other city, after being half-drowned and left to starve, foiled by bureaucracy, and attacked by the auto-immune disease of rampant crime, could stagger to its feet to welcome visitors with a platter of oysters on the half shell and a rousing brass band? Within only a couple of years after Hurricane Katrina in 2005, New Orleans was providing streetcar rides and impromptu parades, riverboat calliopes and sidewalk tap dancers. And a few months after the notorious BP oil spill of 2010 blackened the Louisiana coast, the pre-Mardi Gras parades were rolling through New Orleans neighborhoods and the smell of long loaves baking for po' boy sandwiches was still sweetening the air. When chroniclers look back, the city's ability to be itself — a place that embraces sorrow and joy with equal gusto — even in its hardest of times will become part of its legend. — BY SHAILA DEWAN

FRIDAY

1 Drinks on the Porch 5 p.m.

New Orleans is a state of mind, one acquired most efficiently with an afternoon cocktail. At the bar of the **Columns** (3811 St. Charles Avenue; 504-899-9308; thecolumns.com), an Italianate mansion turned hotel in the Garden District, what must be the South's most inviting porch flirts with the city's grandest thoroughfare. Have a Campari and soda alfresco or step into the bar, with its ornately painted 16-foot ceiling and a circular settee. Both over the top and the tiniest bit down at the heels, the Columns was the perfect backdrop for *Pretty Baby*, Louis Malle's movie about a turn-of-the-century brothel, even though it is a world away from the former red-light district it was meant to evoke.

2 Asian Infusion 7 p.m.

Post-Katrina and post-oil spill, the New Orleans restaurant scene is stronger and more innovative than ever. **Mike's on the Avenue** (628 St. Charles Avenue; 504-523-7600; mikesontheavenue.com; $$$), which

opened in 2010, is one good example, melding Asian and Hawaiian food influences with the flavors of Louisiana. Some of its playful offerings have included a sushi box that includes a Cajun crab roll and duck with shiitake mushrooms, brown rice, and chunks of Cajun ham and andouille sausage.

3 Jazz and Books 9 p.m.

In 1768, the French settlers of New Orleans ran an unloved Spanish governor out of town and had a street named after them for their trouble: Frenchmen Street. Today, the street stands in happy rebellion against another takeover: the tourist swarm in the French Quarter on the other side of Esplanade. On Frenchmen, both good music and friendly local people spill out of the clubs and into the streets. For serious jazz head to **Snug Harbor** (626 Frenchmen; 504-949-0696; snugjazz.com), where members of the Marsalis or Neville dynasties make frequent appearances. A more casual, and funkier, atmosphere reigns across the street at the **Spotted Cat** (623 Frenchmen; 206-337-3273; spottedcatmusicclub.com). At **d.b.a.** (618 Frenchmen; 504-942-3731; dbabars.com/dbano), live music coexists with a long list of single-malt Scotches. When your ears need a rest, stop in at **Faubourg Marigny Art & Books** (600 Frenchmen; 504-947-3700; fabonfrenchmen.com), where you can find books about New Orleans, gay and lesbian literature, postcards, and the lowdown on the town from Otis Fennell, the owner, who stays open "as late as it takes."

OPPOSITE The French Quarter, New Orleans.

RIGHT The city's Social Aid and Pleasure Clubs not only provide jazz funerals, but parade through New Orleans neighborhoods on Sunday afternoons.

SATURDAY

4 *The Real Story* 10 a.m.

Much of the history of New Orleans musicians, plus other largely African-American New Orleans traditions like skeleton gangs, jazz parades, and the Mardi Gras Indians with their handmade, proto-Vegas costumes, has been lovingly collected by Sylvester Francis. His **Backstreet Cultural Museum** (1116 St. Claude Avenue; 504-522-4806; backstreetmuseum.org)

ABOVE Casual night life at the Spotted Cat.

BELOW Kermit Ruffins, a New Orleans favorite. Check the listings to see where the top acts are playing.

is tucked inside a former funeral home in the Tremé district. In a city where history is still happening, little shrines like Backstreet are legion and their sole proprietors, like Francis, are oracles.

5 *Potions and Scents* 11 a.m.

The **New Orleans Pharmacy Museum** (514 Chartres Street; 504-565-8027; pharmacymuseum.org) might sound a bit dry, but this 1823 town house is like a concentrated version of the city itself, with exhibits on not only apothecary supplies and soda fountains, but also hangover remedies, voodoo potions, absinthe, opium, and "questionable medical practices." You can also get some good souvenir ideas in the neighborhood. A "rare and intoxicating tobacco" called perique, grown only in a small tract of land in one parish in Louisiana, is available at the nearby **Cigar Factory** (415 Decatur Street; 504-568-1003; cigarfactoryneworleans.com). Vetivert, an earthy scent the museum says was favored by Creole women, can be purchased around the corner at **Hové Parfumeur**, as a perfume, soap, or simply bundles of root (824 Royal Street; 504-525-7827; hoveparfumeur.com).

6 *Eat Your Po' Boy* Noon

New Orleans is called the Crescent City because of the Mississippi River's snaky pinch, which also has made it hard to discern north, south, east, and west.

The custom instead is this: you can go toward the lake, toward the river, upriver or downriver. Starting in Jackson Square, which looks to this day like a Mary Poppins movie set, stroll toward the lake. Go all the way to Rampart Street and turn right. That's downriver. Cross Esplanade, continue one block, and enter the bright orange convenience store. That's heaven. Also known as the **Rampart Street Food Store** (1700 North Rampart Street; 504-944-7777; $). Order the shrimp po' boy on French bread and join all the other people, some still in their bedroom slippers, waiting for their po' boy fix.

7 *After the Flood* 1 p.m.

Katrina couldn't kill New Orleans, but it's a smaller city now, with fewer people living in the lowest coastal neighborhoods. See the hurricane's remaining effects and hear what made the city so vulnerable by taking a seat on the **Gray Line Katrina Tour** (graylineneworleans.com; 504-569-1401; leaving where Toulouse Street meets the river). Guides will explain how levees were breached, tell how the city's residents were affected in the immediate aftermath, and explain the effects of the loss of coastal wetlands.

ABOVE For every renowned restaurant, there is a beloved neighborhood place. This one is Dick and Jenny's.

PAGE 337 Hové Parfumeur carries Creole scent.

You'll also see the port. If three hours on a bus is too much, find one of the many cab drivers with a tour guide license and negotiate a shorter trip.

8 *Local Fare* 6 p.m.

For every Emeril's, Antoine's, or Brennan's in this city of fine dining, there is a beloved neighborhood restaurant where locals will wait hours for a table. At **Dick and Jenny's** (4501 Tchoupitoulas Street; 504-894-9880; dickandjennys.com), in a rambling Uptown barge-board cottage, the dishes might include savory crawfish and andouille cheesecake, pecan-crusted veal sweetbreads, and salmon with Gewürztraminer beurre blanc. They don't take reservations, so settle in on a porch glider with a cocktail and wait.

9 *The Play List* 9 p.m.

Ask New Orleanians about the night's music offerings and chances are they'll rattle them off from memory (if not, pick up a free copy of *Offbeat* magazine). Listen for the city's top acts—the Rebirth Brass Band, the Hot 8, Kermit Ruffins and the Barbecue Swingers, John Boutté, Troy (Trombone Shorty) Andrews. They play at various venues including the **Maple Leaf Bar** (8316 Oak Street; 504-866-9359; mapleleafbar.com), which has a packed dance floor, pressed-tin walls, and a courtyard perfect for brief respites.

SUNDAY

10 *Ambition* 10 a.m.

The thing to love about **Elizabeth's** (601 Gallier Street; 504-944-9272; elizabeths-restaurant.com) is that somebody there tried to make bacon better. The result is praline bacon—a combination of pecan candy and salty pork. The homely little restaurant in the shadow of the Mississippi River levee keeps them coming at breakfast with dishes like strawberry stuffed French toast and Cajun Bubble and Squeak, combining bacon, cabbage, shrimp, poached eggs, and Hollandaise.

11 *Follow the Music* 1 p.m.

New Orleans is a tribal place, made up of Mardi Gras Indian tribes and krewes, and groups known as Social Aid and Pleasure Clubs, originally formed to provide burial insurance. Now the clubs not only provide jazz funerals, but also mount their own parades, known as second lines, that pass through the city's neighborhoods—often from bar to bar—on Sunday afternoons. The Nine Times, the Original Four, the Mahogany Ladies—those are but a few of the clubs that try to one-up one another with color-coded haberdashery and the city's best brass bands. If you have some extra time, get a "route sheet" for the second line (the idea is to follow it, not stand at the side and watch it). To that end, begin asking around early—Sylvester Francis at the Backstreet might let you in on it—or sidle up to your bartender or door-man. Because, as anyone in New Orleans will tell you, the best way to hear a brass band is to dance down the street behind it.

THE BASICS

Fly into Louis Armstrong New Orleans International Airport

Travel on foot and by streetcar.

The Roosevelt New Orleans
123 Baronne Street
therooseveltneworleans.com
504-648-1200
$$$
New Orleans landmark, formerly the Fairmont; renovated after Katrina damage and reopened in 2009.

Olivier House
828 Toulouse Street
504-525-8456
olivierhouse.com
$$
A New Orleans classic with a maze-like series of interior courtyards.

Lookout Inn
833 Poland Avenue
504-947-8188
lookoutneworleans.com
$
Four suites and a saltwater pool.

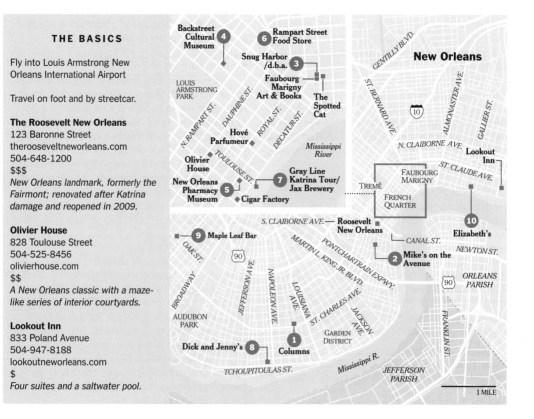

Indexes

Additional photo credits: The Colonial Williamsburg Foundation, 34; Town of Cary/photo by Roger May, 42; Dan Dry, 128; Gallo Images/Getty Images, 8; Hoberman Collection/Universal Images Group/Getty Images, 2; Lonely Planet Images/Getty Images 122; Nashville Convention and Visitors Bureau, 134; Richard Nowitz/Getty Images, 4; Visit Savannah (VisitSavannah.com), 52–53; State of Tennessee, 140, 143; Virginia Beach Convention and Visitors Bureau, 38.

Acknowledgments

We would like to thank everyone at *The New York Times* and at TASCHEN who contributed to the creation of this book.

For the book project itself, special recognition must go to Nina Wiener and Eric Schwartau at TASCHEN, the dedicated editor and assistant behind the scenes; to Natasha Perkel, the *Times* artist whose clear and elegantly crafted maps make the itineraries comprehensible; to Phyllis Collazo of the *Times* staff, whose photo editing gave the book its arresting images; and to Olimpia Zagnoli, whose illustrations and illustrated maps enliven every article and each regional introduction.

Guiding the deft and artful transformation of newspaper material to book form at TASCHEN were Marco Zivny, the book's designer; Josh Baker, the art director; and Jennifer Patrick, production manager. Also at TASCHEN, David Martinez, Jessica Sappenfeld, Anna-Tina Kessler, Kirstin Plate and Janet Kim provided production assistance, and at the *Times*, Heidi Giovine helped at critical moments. Craig B. Gaines copy-edited the manuscript.

But the indebtedness goes much further back. This book grew out of the work of all of the editors, writers, photographers, and *Times* staff people whose contributions and support for the weekly "36 Hours" column built a rich archive over many years.

For this legacy, credit must go first to Stuart Emmrich, who created the column in 2002 and then refined the concept and guided its development over eight years, first as the *Times* Escapes editor and then as Travel editor. Without his vision, there would be no "36 Hours."

Great thanks must go to all of the writers and photographers whose work appears in the book, both *Times* staffers and freelancers.

And a legion of *Times* editors behind the scenes made it all happen, and still do.

Danielle Mattoon, who took over as Travel editor in 2010, has brought her steady hand to "36 Hours," and found time to be supportive of this book as well.

Suzanne MacNeille, now the column's direct editor, and her predecessors Jeff Z. Klein and Denny Lee have all superbly filled the role of finding and working with writers, choosing and assigning destinations, and assuring that the weekly product would entertain and inform readers while upholding *Times* journalistic standards. The former Escapes editors Amy Virshup and Mervyn Rothstein saw the column through many of its early years, assuring its consistent quality.

The talented *Times* photo editors who have overseen images and directed the work of the column's photographers include Lonnie Schlein, Jessica DeWitt, Gina Privitere, Darcy Eveleigh, Laura O'Neill, Chris Jones, and the late John Forbes. The newspaper column's design is the work of the *Times* art director Rodrigo Honeywell.

Among the many editors on the *Times* Travel and Escapes copy desks who have kept "36 Hours" at its best over the years, three who stand out are Florence Stickney, Steve Bailey, and Carl Sommers. Editors of the column on the *New York Times* web site have been Alice Dubois, David Allan, Miki Meek, Allison Busacca, and Danielle Belopotosky. Much of the fact-checking, that most invaluable and unsung of skills, was in the hands of Rusha Haljuci, Nick Kaye, Anna Bahney, and George Gustines.

Finally, we must offer a special acknowledgment to Benedikt Taschen, whose longtime readership and interest in the "36 Hours" column led to the partnership of our two companies to produce this book.

— BARBARA IRELAND AND ALEX WARD

Copyright © 2013 *The New York Times*. All Rights Reserved.

Editor Barbara Ireland
Project management Alex Ward
Photo editor Phyllis Collazo
Maps Natasha Perkel
Spot illustrations and region maps Olimpia Zagnoli
Editorial coordination Nina Wiener and Eric Schwartau
Art direction Marco Zivny and Josh Baker
Layout and design Marco Zivny
Production Jennifer Patrick

To stay informed about upcoming TASCHEN titles, please request our magazine at www.taschen.com/magazine or write to TASCHEN, Hohenzollernring 53, D–50672 Cologne, Germany, contact@taschen.com. We will be happy to send you a free copy of our magazine which is filled with information about all of our books.

© 2013 TASCHEN GmbH
Hohenzollernring 53, D–50672 Köln, www.taschen.com

ISBN 978-3-8365-4202-9 Printed in China

TRUST *THE NEW YORK TIMES* WITH YOUR NEXT 36 HOURS

"The ultimate weekend planner for the literate by the literate — where even Oklahoma City can be as alluring as Paris." —AMAZON READER REVIEW

AVAILABLE IN *THE NEW YORK TIMES* 36 HOURS SERIES

150 WEEKENDS IN THE USA & CANADA*

Weekends on the road. The ultimate travel guide to the USA and Canada

125 WEEKENDS IN EUROPE

(Re)discovering Europe: dream weekends with practical itineraries from Paris to Perm

* also available for iPad

USA & CANADA REGION BY REGION

| NORTHEAST | SOUTHEAST | MIDWEST & GREAT LAKES | SOUTHWEST & ROCKY MOUNTAINS | WEST COAST |

FOR NEWS ON UPCOMING BOOKS IN THIS SERIES, VISIT WWW.TASCHEN.COM

SOUTH EAST